Narratives, Musings, and Memories

by

John N. DeFoor

NARRATIVES MUSINGS AND MEMORIES

First edition. July 2, 2024.

ISBN: 979-8224029952

Written by John N DeFoore Sr..

Table of Contents

Acknowledgements

First, I want to thank my beloved wife Marion Sue DeFoore for allowing me to use her exquisite artwork for the cover design of this book.

Her care for me all the years of our married life, and especially these last, much more challenging years, has been amazing, and far beyond what I could ever have expected from anyone.

She would say it's just been her duty and a labor of love, but for me it's truly been life-saving. Thank you, my love, for your care and your love for me.

In addition, this book would not have been possible without my friend and editor, Ernestine Hass.

I must extend my deepest gratitude to her for her immense patience and expertise in editing, correcting, and improving this book. Her excellent language skills have made this book more interesting and accurate.

Thank you from the bottom of my heart for your unwavering support and invaluable contributions to this book.

John DeFoore was born in 1919 in the small town of Sidon, Mississippi. He grew up surrounded by cotton fields and dense forests. He left home at age 17 and went to work with a highway construction group. He finished high school, started college, and entered the Army before WWII began. He served seven years, enlisting as a private first class and being discharged as a major. He was in the infantry and saw service in New Guinea, the Netherlands East Indies, and the Philippines. He was awarded the Bronze Star during an amphibious landing on Morotai Island.

After the war, John was ordained as a Baptist minister and graduated from Mississippi College with a Bachelor of Science degree and Southern Baptist Theological Seminary with a Master of Theology degree. He further studied at New College in Edinburgh, Scotland, Princeton, Harvard, and the Jungian Institute in Zurich, Switzerland.

He served as a missionary in Alaska for five years and then pastored in Mississippi, Alabama, and Texas for over 30 years. At 65, he began his second career as a counselor and international business consultant and retired from this practice at 98. He and his wife, Marion Sue, live in Boerne, Texas. He is the father of four sons.

At 105 years old, John still spends his days writing and reading. Since retiring, he has written more than a dozen books.

Short Stories

Uncle Alec

CHAPTER ONE

His name was Uncle Alec.
        "Young Massa...
dis hear
is da way
hit tis."
And slowly
carefully
he explained,
All the accomplished wisdom
of a thousand generations
of toil and trouble, slavery, and suffering—-
jungles, fields, farms, life, and living
poured through the funnel
of a compassionate heart—-
to teach
to instruct
to guide
and direct
his charge—-
"Dis little white boy"
through the pathways of the world
that he would travel.
He taught me.
He taught me while I sat by his side,
walked down the road, or
worked in the cotton fields.

How to chop wood.
How to file a saw.
The way to milk a cow.
Say "Sir to de mens" and "Mam to de womens."
"Drive de nail dis a way."
"Don t pay no tentshon to dat snake, he aint bad."
"Kerful, rat chear, dont hurt yo self."
"De suns goin down. We bes go home."
His aged, slender frame—
crippled by an earlier stroke—
did not alter the strength of a giant—
(Ancient Mars and Thor stood in awe when
they stood in his shadow.)
There was nothing he could not do—
there was nothing he did not know—
God stood at his shoulder for support.
I needed no picture of "Iron John."

When I stepped outside my back door to take his hand, it was not yet light. The walk to the cotton field was relatively short. We arrived. Everyone else was already there preparing for the day.

Shaking out the sacks, placing the water buckets, tying the lunch buckets in the trees, and then walking to the cotton rows to be picked.

All this is done with the soft and melodious moan—
of a hymn sung by angels—

> *"Go down, Moses-*
> *Oh Lord, we come dis mornin – knee bowed*
> *and body bent-*
> *Swing low, sweet chariot-*
> *In dat great gittin up mornin."*

through the ancient throats of God's people
waiting to face the day "pickin' cotton."

Softly, the golden rising sun placed halos on the battered, faded straw hats of the men, circled round by the rag-tied coverings for the women.

Without a sound, the bent backs and hasty hands started
Pickin' cotton.
The day had begun.
We worked.
We worked because the work needed to be done.
We worked because we were laborers.
We worked because we were hired and paid.

CHAPTER TWO

Her name was Lizzie.

She was my "mother." My birth mother taught school all day and worked in my uncle's general store until it closed each night at ten pm. My real mother was Lizzie.

Lizzie was at home; in charge—cooking, cleaning,

supervising, and doing everything that the mother of a family would do.

She disciplined all five of the children in the family.

She taught us about life.

She fed us.

She spanked us.

She loved and nurtured all of the children, none of whom were born of her body,

but all of us had been born of her soul.

Her skin was dark brown, but her soul was lily white. The color of the skin was less important than the beauty of her maternal care.

I do not know if she was ever paid for her services. There is a family tradition that when my father was dying of cancer and in the hospital, he sent for Lizzie. The story is that he told Lizzie she had to stay with us until all the children were grown. If she did not, he would come back and "haint" her.

She stayed.

There were times when our family was short of food. Lizzie found some somewhere. I distinctly remember overhearing this conversation in the kitchen one day:

Lizzie: (To Uncle Alec) "Old man, der aint nuthin in dis house fer me to cook. You git outta here and find me some vittles so I can feed dis family."

Uncle Alec: "I be back in a little while."

He left. Sometime later I saw him walking into the back door of the house. He had an arm full of turnip greens, a few tomatoes, and several ears of corn.

I do not know where or how he got them. I did not ask. We had food. These two people were making sure the family was fed.

Swimming in the river was strictly forbidden by mother. We did it anyway. All summer long, Lizzie would ask us at supper time: "You been in dat river?" We always said "No." She knew we were not telling the truth but she felt responsible for asking. Nothing more was said.

Lizzie was there. She was always there. She never took vacations or holidays that I can ever remember.

• • • •

(IN WORLD WAR II, ALL four boys entered the service. My youngest brother, Jud, was the last to enlist, and he chose the Navy. He left for training on a Thursday afternoon. Lizzie left the next day. She moved to Greenwood and got married the following week.)

CHAPTER THREE

Lizzie always left after supper. Uncle Alec came and stayed with us until Mother came home. Usually, she came around ten or ten thirty in the evening.

The four boys were rowdy. We had pillow fights and races around the room. One of our favorite things was to climb up to the wooden head of the bed and dive into the pile of quilts and blankets on the bed. We played like it was a swimming pool.

It usually took a while for us to exhaust our energy before we could lie down and sleep. Uncle Alec would always get the Bible and read it out loud to us. We did not listen, but that did not matter to him. His broken glasses lay at an angle across his nose, and the Bible lay askew across his only good leg.

He read aloud with the request, "Now y'all listen, young men. Dis here is de word of de Lord."

He read. When he came to a word he could not pronounce, he spelled the word and kept on reading. He read every night with the hope that we would hear and understand the message in some strange way. Often, he would stop and pray. I remember him calling our names in prayer. He would pray for us and then continue to read the Bible.

Usually, we were asleep when Mother came home. I think Uncle Alec was also sleeping most of the time. My mother would wake him up and he would leave and go to his own house.

The next day he was always there. He did all the jobs around the house that needed to be done and he always watched us to make sure we did not get hurt.

CHAPTER FOUR

I am sure he knew he was black.

I do not think he ever felt inferior or cautious as he took care of our family.

At the same time, I felt he knew he was the father and the head of the family. He carried a personal responsibility for each of us. This man also carried a personal and special place in my heart.

On the afternoons when I played baseball on the school ground I would always see him in the distance. He would come and watch me play but never with the crowd. He would stand far off and alone, but he was there.

It was the same way on Sunday morning when we were getting ready for church. He would be there in the house helping us get dressed and making sure our shoes were shined. When we left for church he disappeared and returned in the early afternoon.

There were times when he took me to his church on Sunday afternoon. His church was an aging building on the edge of a cotton field, sagging at one corner and badly in need of paint. But it was his church.

He would take me into the building and place me in a window. The admonition was always the same: "Now you sit rat here. Dont you git down cause ifen you git on dat flo you mought get stomped."

The worship service started. Several of the men preached. Some could not read, so they had a woman read the Bible for them, and they repeated the phrases as they were read. There were varying responses from the congregation like: "Preach on, Brother... Praise De Lord,... and Dats right, Reverend."

Occasionally. there was dancing in the aisles. It was a slow movement, almost hypnotic to watch and always in harmony with the soft singing of the church. The singing was rhythmic. The sounds were soft and low. There was a lot of repetition in the words. The singing was mournful. It was plaintive. The combined voices formed a chorus that was a cry, a wail, a vocal heartbeat that seemed to come from the depths of every human soul in the room.

The music resonated deeply in my heart, and I can remember at times joining in the singing. It was safe for me to do that because I felt totally accepted and safe because everyone knew I was"Brother Alec's little white boy."

This was my first experience at worship. I knew. I felt. I sensed a Presence, other-worldly-out-of-body-ethereal that spoke to the deepest levels of my heart. I learned to call it God.

When the service was ended Uncle Alec would come and get me from the window. Several times I remember being asleep and he would pick me up in his arms and take me home.

Then the day had ended. I was safe. I was home.

CHAPTER FIVE

· · · ·

THE WINTER NIGHT WAS bitter cold. Our family had gone to bed early in an effort to stay warm. Fierce and freezing winds blew at almost storm speed around our home on the riverside in the Mississippi Delta. Snow had come with the wind and it wrapped the house in a blanket of white. The plants and trees were encased in the winter's embrace of frost and snow.

Finally, our family was all in bed and settled for a long winter night's sleep. We were interested only in staying warm for the night.

Not long after we were in bed I heard someone knocking loudly at the back door. I could not imagine who it would be. On such a bad dark night who in the world would be knocking for entrance into our house?

I crawled out of bed, went down the long dark hall to the back door. Not sure of myself I opened the door very slowly. To my utter surprise I saw Uncle Alec standing there with an armload of wood. He immediately said, "Stand aside young Massa. I done brung some extra wood cuz dis here nite, hits gonna be bad cold."

He then brought in three armloads of wood for each of the three fireplaces. Then he turned to me and said, "Young Massa, you go back to bed now. Eva thang is goan be alright."

I went back to bed. I thought of this angel coming to our house to make sure we had wood and were warm. At that moment I knew everything would be all right. I felt as if God were taking care of my family and me. Then, I thought about Uncle Alec walking through the snow going back to his cabin.

I crawled back into my bed and felt the safety of the home-made quilts. I had the conscious thought in the dark embrace of the cold and the storm: "Someone cares for me. Someone is looking after me and my family. Thank God for Uncle Alec."

CHAPTER SIX

"**D**is here pickin' cotton, hits a man's job. I know day bees a lotta women in de field but hit is sho nuff a man's job. Dats jess de way hit is."

• • • •

WE WERE IN THE COTTON field just before dawn and we picked until the sun went down. There were usually twice as many women as there were men. Everyone had a water jug that was carried in the sack. Occasionally someone brought food in a tin "molasses" bucket but not often.

I got the same instructions every morning: "You always looks fo de white and dats de way yo hans move. You don t never look back. You don t never look up. You jes pick. You always looks ahead and you keep yo hands a movin. Don never stop yo hans fum movin."

All the instruction came amid the sound of the heavy sack being dragged on the Delta soil, the crickets' call, and the distant lowing of a cow.

A soft curtain of music always hung over the field of workers. Every single person sang. The singing was not only vocal. It was much more. It was more than words. It was a blanket of harmony and color that floated over the cotton fields punctuated by occasional soft laughter and an occasional cough. The singing was prayer. It was petition. It was praise. It was an ancient cry and an audible heartthrob.

The plantation manager or owner was "boss." His coming and going was always watched for very carefully. He usually rode a horse and visited the different fields where the cotton was being picked. When he came everyone picked a little faster and moved a little quicker.

There was always a dominant person in the crowd of cotton pickers who was the leader. This individual earned the position of leader because he could pick the most cotton in one single day. He was the one who watched for the boss.

When the boss appeared on his horse the leader of the group would spot him and indicate his position. The boss was referred to as "Lightening."

I heard the message: "Lightning in de east" or "lightning in de south" to indicate the direction of approach of the boss.

The plantation manager would ride up to the bunch of cotton pickers and greet them briefly and he would ride away. As soon as he disappeared you could hear the message, "He gone. He don gone." Then we returned to our normal pace of picking the cotton.

There were small buildings placed in various locations in the fields. When the cotton sacks were weighed, the cotton was dumped in the "cotton house." Later it was transferred to a wagon and taken to the cotton gin.

Of course, everyone had to take an occasional bathroom break. When this was necessary, the person would simply drop his sack and go to the nearby woods. Those near him would drag his sack and pick the cotton off his row and put it in his sack. "So, he don't get leff behind."

The setting sun marked the end of the day. We all moved to the cotton house; we "weighed up," dumped our cotton in the cotton house, and went home. Before we left we made sure the boss had listed in his book the number of pounds we had picked that day. Another day had come and gone.

CHAPTER SEVEN

• • • •

HE TOLD ME STORIES. He entertained me. At the same time, he taught me about life. As always, he would begin the stories with the words: "Now hear dis. Dis here is de exact way hit was. Hit was jes like dis hear."

"Der was dis man what had de job a turnin de railroad bridge which wer across de river. Dis here bridge let de train go cross de river, but when de boats come down de river de bridge, she hadda be turn so de boat, he could go by.

"When de boat cum, de man he look at he watch so he make sho de train woudnt comin. De train he don stop so de bridge, he mus be strait.

"One day de boat he come and de capin in de boat he say, 'Turn de bridge.'

"But de man say 'I cant turn de bridge cause de train, he comin now.' De steamboat capin he say 'Turn de bridge cause you got time.'

"But de train man; he mad and he say, 'Turn de bridge cause Ize in a hurry and I got to go thru.'

"Den the man, he turn de bridge, and hear come de train! De man he cane do nuttin cause de boat hit in de middle er de bridge and de train hits a comin and a comin and a comin...

"...and din de train run off de track and hit de boat and de boat she done sank and all de peoples in de train an in de boat don drowned in de river.

"Den de man what turn de bridge he cry, an he cry, an he cry, an he say, 'O efen I jes hadna done it! Efen I jes hadna done it! Efen I jes hadna done it!'

"But he done it."

It was then that Uncle Alec would look at me, shake his head, and say: "Young Massa, don never do nuthin whats gonna make you say, 'Efen I jes hadna done dat.' Don never do dat. Don never do dat."

I have never forgotten the man who turned the bridge for the boat.

CHAPTER EIGHT

I remember another story which he told over and over. It went like this:

"Der wuz dis man what work in de sto. He work eva day and when it git dark he clos de sto, and he got in he car and he go home. He do dis eva day.

"Sepn dis man he wer a bad man. He neva treated people rite. He were a bad, bad man. One day he waz on de way home an he see a log in de road an he don stop. He jes say I run over de log. So, he rund de car over de log but what he don know is dis aint no log. Hits a snake. Hit wer a big black snake.

"N de man he look back, and hear cum de snake. 'An de snake he et up de man, and den he et up de whole car, too. He did. Dat snake he so mad he et de man…n den he et de car—sho nuff. An dats what de snake he done."

"Now young man don you be bad. Don nevah be bad."

CHAPTER NINE

THE MUSIC—THE SINGING defies description.

I heard it the first time in the church. I also heard it in the cotton fields.

The music was more than singing. It was more than harmony or melody. It was even more than a combination of both.

The music was somewhat like a cry that pushed itself beyond the boundaries of words and notes. It came from the depths of a human soul. It came in the form of harmonious feelings pouring out of a cauldron of birthing, growing, living, working, and dying. It was deeper.

Each note was a symphony of feelings that had no words or phrases, and when it emerged, it screamed and cried and moaned and begged and pleaded to be heard.

The singing was always soft and sacred except for the times it grew in volume in order to be given a place in the heart of the hearer. When it emerged from the heart and the mouth of the singer, it floated on the air like the smoke from the cooking stoves on the small tenement houses where the singers lived.

Once voiced it took on a presence all its own. Carrying passion. Conveying pain. Expressing hope. Like silent screams from a wounded being it forced a hearing... as if the heart had to be heard, as if the melody demanded an audience, as if the sound had a character and personality all its own-it came.

I listened. I heard deeper than tears. A sense of awe, a sense of wonder, an emotion that sprang from the bowels of the earth poured forth from a human heart that cried out for a hearing.

I could not cry. I did not moan. I did not even wince as I listened.

I have never before or since heard the screaming pleas of humanity. There was always a leader who composed the notes and words as the song was sung. It also had its own language and its own harmony never before expressed until the one moment when the singer gave birth to the new message.

CHAPTER TEN

• • • •

IT STARTED TO RAIN.

Uncle Alec and I moved to the small "cotton house" that stood in the middle of the very large cotton field. We both threw our cotton sacks inside and then crawled in after them.

The huge billows of freshly picked cotton provided a warm and inviting place for us to rest. I was snuggled down and sleepy, but then I heard Uncle Alec start to talk.

He was staring out the open door and watching the rain. He did not look at me. It seemed he was deep in thought, and then I heard him say:

"Young Massa, sometime life–hit bees hard. You is gonna find de road is hot and dusty on dim days. You may not be able ta find a friend when you needs dem. Dat road hit can get pretty lonesome some time.

"Hits times like dis you jess lean on de Lord. He will be dere and he will help you. He dont never leave you by yo'sef. Dis is wen you pray. Now de friens day come and day go. Sometimes day is wid you, and sometime day is gone, but de Lawd he don never leave you. You jes hole on, and hole on, and hole on to de Lawd.

"Doan nevah give up, Young Massa. De road hit gits mighty dark on some days. But you don nevah giv up. You jes keep a walkin and walkin and den you see bettah days and bettah times."

I listened.

Snuggling down deeper in the cotton still warm from the sun I watched the face and the hands of this black giant. With his hands he picked at the cotton. He pulled its long fibers between his fingers as he talked and stared at the darkening sky outside.

"An den yo body hits gonna get old jes like mine," he continued, "But jes don you nevermind. Hit aint bad to be old. Hits jes hard. But de Lord he stays wich ya. He don never leave. He is always dar."

Slowly I drifted off to sleep, bathed in the melodious harmony of that beautiful voice that wrapped me round in a blanket of safety I can never forget.

The rain on the roof sounded a soft benediction to the warm and loving prayers of my surrogate father.

CHAPTER ELEVEN

THE MIRACLE OF THE man—Uncle Alec.

In trying to tell the story of this simple human being I find myself searching for a title. None seems to be adequate. I would not insult his memory by trying to idealize him nor would I want to downplay the dignity of who he was and who he still is in my mind.

Memory has its own looking glass and it does not always conform to our boundaries of reality and accuracy. Having said that, I found the courage to put into words the way I remember him and what he meant to me.

To me he was a giant notwithstanding the fact that he was barely five feet tall. He was as strong as Hercules; yet, a stroke had left him crippled and dragging his right arm and right leg whenever he walked. He was bigger than life; he was wiser than space; he was more patient than time, and older than history.

But to me he was "Uncle Alec."

None of this registered to me when I was a child. Nothing registered other than the fact that he was always "There." He was present. He was always present and no one could ignore the authenticity of his being. His presence in my world spoke volumes unhindered by words or sounds or movement.

I do not recall his eyes. Except to register the fact that he always seemed to know where I was. Deeper than this, it seemed he always knew what I was thinking. There were times when I thought he might be psychic. I never felt ignored or invisible in his presence.

All the years and all the miles that I have travelled and lived since I have been separated from this man—they all have not separated me from a presence and a knowledge that I was important–I am significant–I am valued and I am loved.

Time does not stand still. Nothing remains the same. It was inevitable that we should be separated physically. I left this small town and went to war and then one day I got a simple message from my mother.

"We buried Uncle Alec today."

On the other side of the globe, I felt a loss. I knew a part of me had ceased to exist and that a bigger part of me had been strengthened.

I was still in the middle of the war. The insanity of the carnage; the senselessness of the killing, and the endless trail of destruction did not end. In some strange way I felt a comfort—a reassurance—in the message that he was at rest. I crawled back in my fox hole and cried.

The lessons he taught did not die. The instructions he gave did not leave me. The quiet comfort of his presence still spanned the miles from home to remind me of God and love and life and meaning.

He was buried back in Mississippi.

He still lived in my heart.

CHAPTER TWELVE

. . . .

THE PRESENCE:

(This is introspection. Looking back, I do not see or understand how I survived childhood. There was a lot of death in the small town where I began my life. I buried friends. I have often wondered why and how I survived. From some source I found strength. At the time I was not aware of its source but it was there.)

I never knew my father. The very few whispers of him that survived as memories are very fleeting. I have treasured them in fleeting moments with faltering memories. They are very dim.

But, on reflection, I have found that there was always a presence in my life. I do not know if it was God, Uncle Alec, fate, or happenstance. I find it hard to identity it or give it a name.

After writing about this man Uncle Alec, I have come to understand that he was the force in my life and in my childhood that made me survive.

There was no emotional support in my childhood from a mother figure or a father figure. My grandfather was a remote influence even though I tried to establish a relationship with him. My support—my security—my stabilizing force had to come from this one individual. There was no one else.

I do not know, looking back, how I did the things I did as a child. I am surprised when I recall the decisions and actions I took as a child. There must have been someone encouraging me. It could only have been one person.

. . . .

(THIS IS VERY HARD TO write, but I felt I had to include it in this writing. My mother beat me. It seemed that she did this every day. It was more than a whipping. It was a beating. Sometimes she used her fists. Sometimes she used a stick. But my entire childhood is cursed with the memories of these beatings. She also beat my sister, Frances, but not as often as she beat me.)

I do not know how I found the energy or the will to live and do the work that I remember doing to keep the household going. It seems to me—-could I possibly have been seven or eight years old and doing the chores at home? The memories are very distinct: chopping wood; milking the cow; gathering eggs; feeding pigs; working the garden and picking cotton (at first with a flour sack-very small).

I remember distinctly hauling cotton bales when I was twelve years old because that same year I joined the Boy Scouts. Cotton bales at that time weighed five to six hundred pounds. I still do not know how I handled the large bales of cotton. I rolled them down the ramp at the gin; loaded them onto a wagon; took them to the railroad platform and unloaded them there and got five cents for each bale I moved. (Sometimes I made another five cents loading them from the railroad platform into the box cars on the train.)

As often as I could I worked at the sawmill firing the boiler. I hauled slabs cut off the logs, from the saw to the boiler and fired the boiler. I made one dollar each day I worked there and promptly gave it to Mother.

I remember several times playing baseball with the "big boys" when I was twelve. One time I distinctly remember "getting a hit." How I found the courage to do that I do not know.

From Uncle Alec I got the distinct message that I was a man and that I could do anything that had to be done. It was rarely verbalized; rather it was communicated in his presence and in his confident support. This is supposed to be the message from every father to a son. It is the reason children are born to parents.

Looking back the only memory of anything encouraging, or supportive, or helpful was the presence of Uncle Alec. He has always "there." Or he was always nearby.

Or else I would never have survived childhood.

I thank God for that man in my life.

Skier Lost in the Snow
CHAPTER ONE

. . . .

BURIED IN A SNOWBANK for no reason. I had no sense of falling—no loss of balance—no sensation to indicate I was falling—I , the expert top-notch skier in the area, here I was topsy-survey in the snow. I chuckled to myself and actually laughed just a little before I tried to stand.

I was half erect before I realized one of the ski straps had broken, in fact I had lost one ski. I turned my head and saw the errant ski sticking in the snow in easy reach. I chuckled to myself and realized I had not checked the bindings before I hit the slopes, and I always, always, always did that before I went to the mountain. I took just a minute to check the sun to see if I could make another run before the lift closed.

While attempting to replace the broken binding someone stopped near me and asked, "You OK?" I turned and saw Norah, my younger sister, who had come with me to the mountain. Norah was one of the bright spots in my life, and we both laughed when we were on the way again. I skied behind her, picked her up, and put her on my shoulders. I loved to do this, and she loved it even more.

On the way down, I felt my phone buzzing but waited to answer it until I unloaded at the bottom. I called Mom when I saw her number and heard her say, "Your dad hasn't been feeling well lately so we decided to go to the clinic for a checkup."

I walked over to meet Norah and we both decided to go to the clinic to talk with Dad and see what the doctor had to say. As we walked into the clinic Norah hit me on the shoulder and said, "I will race you down Big Blue this afternoon." I said "Good deal" and opened the door to let her enter before me.

We waited just a minute for Mom and then we all three went to the doctor's lounge where we could talk with the doctor. The doctor came in and pulled his chair out in front of us. He was very soft-spoken and talked quietly and said, "I have some news that is not so good, so I want you to listen very carefully and ask any questions that come to your mind. I have all the time you will need so that there is need to hurry."

Then he turned to Mom and said, "Your husband has a very serious heart problem. We discovered it several years ago, but he was insistent that absolutely no one else be told. I urged him to talk to you, but he insisted that no one else should know. "I would like for him to remain in the hospital for a few days for some tests." Mother went over to Norah and sat down by her side and said nothing.

We all continued to sit there in silence but soon left for home. We were just a little shaken by what had happened, of course. I was trying to be calm and not blow my cool before Norah because I did not want to frighten her. I did not have to worry long because as soon as she hit the couch she was asleep. Mother went to the kitchen, so I went in and pretended to be looking for food in the refrigerator. When I turned around, she had fixed me a sandwich and placed it on the table.

I sat down and said, "Would you like to tell me what you are thinking, young Lady." She immediately sat down at the table and started sobbing.

It was that exact moment when my father, who had talked the doctor into letting him come home, walked into the room, and said, "Would someone please tell me when the funeral is scheduled. I have never seen such a bedraggled, despondent, beat-down crowd. If you don't mind, I think I'll go down to Joe's bar and see if anyone has heard a good joke lately."

And he started singing, "Happy Days are Here Again." With that he grabbed Mom, picked her up and began to dance across the kitchen. So, I grabbed Norah and began to dance as everyone began to laugh.

It changed the entire family immediately and everyone hugged my Dad. He said, just a little loud, "Listen, you bunch of crazies, I am going to die, but not today and so are each of you, and I did not have to stay two days in the hospital. Got out on good behavior! I hope I won't die today. So, let's save the tears for funeral if you don't mind."

We all applauded, and the laughter returned to the room. Mother started to prepare the evening meal and Dad and I went to the ping pong table. Norah pushed Mom aside and started taking something out of the oven. She was singing "Somewhere over the Rainbow." Soon, we were at the table, and everyone was talking.

It was almost time for me to leave for my fall semester in college and I could not wait to get to med school. I had the feeling that my father was ready for me to be back in school also. He had taught a good while in the med school but retired early because of health problems. Several weeks passed and I was on the road to school. I had been assigned to a dorm and gotten my schedule of classes and labs.

It was good to be on campus again and I immediately called my friend Mary Elizabeth. She was in town even though I knew she was not due for another week. She was one year ahead of me having graduated with honors and earned a fantastic scholarship for a full ride through med school. She was a brain, and I had to struggle to keep up with her.

We talked briefly and she said she was coming over the weekend. She had met my family, and I had met hers but there had been no talk about marriage. I don't know why unless it was because both of us were focused on getting through school. As it stands now, she will finish one year ahead of me.

I went to one of the med buildings and ran into one of my chemistry professors, a Dr. Mullins, with whom I had had several casual conversations. He stopped me and asked if I was busy. Of course, I said, "No," and we went into his classroom.

He sat down at his desk and said, "If you are not too busy and have the time, I would like for you to be one of my lab assistants this next school year."

I was absolutely thrilled and quickly accepted his offer. He told me the student's name who would be senior assistant, and I knew him also and had a good relationship with him. I was more than thrilled as I went back to my dorm.

Back in my room, it suddenly came to me that Mac, my very good friend, had been the lab assistant to Dr. Mullins the year before. I was overpowered with the question of what had happened to Mac, so I called him immediately. He said his father had been killed in an auto-train accident last summer. And he was staying home to take care of the drugstore and support the family. His father had run the drugstore, and it was the main source of family income. He planned to delay his education until his younger sister had finished her high school education.

I was surprised to hear this and immediately went to Dr. Mullins and told him the whole story. We discussed it for quite a while and then I asked Professor Samuels if he would be willing to make Mac his senior assistant and move Fred to a junior position. Dr. Samuels said, "Only if Fred is willing." Dr. Mullins and I talked to Fred and found he would be more than happy to make the change. if it would allow Fred to attend school The deal was done, and Fred was back in his regular place Mac was overjoyed when he heard the wonderful news. We went to talk with his mother, and she was thrilled to get the information. In all this transaction it seemed that Dr. Mullins and I developed a real intimate relationship of trust in each other. School had started and everything was going as it should.

I had not seen or heard from Mary Elizabeth and wondered why she had not called. When we did connect, we decided to go to dinner.

Since she had a car, she picked me up, and I began to tell her everything that had happened. In the middle of my reporting, it suddenly dawned on me that she was not listening and that she was not remotely interested in what I was doing, The awareness hit me like a truck. For a moment, I sat there and then I turned and asked her directly what was on her mind. She looked at me and said, "Robert, the truth is, I am not interested. This summer I met someone else, with whom I seemed to bond instantly."

I was stunned and did not know what to say. I turned and looked out the window and said, "My Friend, I think that message is pretty clear, and I thank you for being straight. If you don't mind, please pullover and I will get out." She said, "Not right here, not downtown."

I said, "Please, right here." To let me out, she pulled over to the curb. I opened the door and got out of the car. That was the end of our relationship. I never saw or heard from her again. I did watch her drive away and waved but she did not look back. I thought, "So much for nothing."

I began to look for a cab, thinking, "Marriage is the pits. Who in the world would anyone want that for a lifestyle?"

$$\bullet \ \ \bullet \ \ \bullet \ \ \bullet$$

$$\bullet \ \ \bullet \ \ \bullet \ \ \bullet$$

I WENT TO MY ROOM AND looked at my wardrobe—-exactly like my father's. I laughed out loud and was embarrassed just listening to myself. I wondered, "What kind of man am I?"

Then, I answered myself and said, "Nothing more than a duplicate of another human being." I was embarrassed and ashamed of myself even with no one watching. Something inside me said, "Life is like that, but eventually we all have to grow up." I stood there a minute surprised at what I was saying to myself. Then I looked around to see who was talking. I was surprised to find no one there.

It was a moment of discovery—-confrontation— or something like that. I stood in place by my bed and turned off the lights because I did not want myself to see me and be embarrassed or ashamed of myself. I did chuckle just a little when I watched myself to see what I was doing.

I did not turn on the lights because there was an explosion of self-discovery in that moment of tears and laughter. I was growing up in a single moment and did not realize it. I stood amid this deluge of emotion and watched my childhood disappear, and an adult strong and tall entered the room to take his place. I did not move or say a word lest the intrusion of my voice destroy the sanctity of the moment.

I went back into the den where Mother and Dad were watching TV. I say, "watching" but both of them were asleep in their chairs with their mouths open. I panicked and felt if I did not get out of the room, I would not be able to breathe. I went straight back to my room. I packed my bag.

I went to my apartment (rarely used) to spend the night. I called the next morning to tell them I had been up late studying and would see them later in the week.

When I shaved that morning and looked in the mirror, I knew that a different person was looking at me. In my bathroom that morning I got down on my knees and thanked God for making me a man and not allowing me to stay a child. I felt it was a moment before God or Jesus Christ as I had come to know him. In fact, I had publicly declared myself a believer in Jesus Christ as the Son of God.

I had grown up, without thought or planning until I realized it was God leading me in a new direction for my life. I felt very strange to realize that someone else was directing my life. I never dreamed this when I became a Christian but everything in me said, "This is the right way. Go-ahead."

CHAPTER TWO

THE VERY NEXT DAY I got a call from THE EDISON COMPANY in upstate New York, with whom I had had correspondence. They were wanting to know if I would consider a study-fellowship,(subject field to be determined). Things were happening so fast in my life, I felt dizzy, but it was all good–so good I could not turn back.

I was in their office two weeks later signing a two-year study fellowship agreement. (I found out later that they had contacted the school for recommendations and both Dr. Mullins and Dr. Samuels had recommended me as "The best in the school.")

Needless to say, I was thrilled and speechless. Mary Elizabeth called to say congratulations and I thanked her, but we talked no further. I had no desire for conversation with her anymore.

Things began to move rapidly. I received a message from EDISON telling me the address of my townhouse and asking if there was anything else they could do to make my move easier.

I moved in and found my workplace easily. When Mom and Dad came for a quick visit, they were both very proud but, needless to say, not as much as I. I was a new person and realized more every day that I was an adult and free. The realization kept bursting into my consciousness.

The strangest thing ever happened to me that day. I was out early jogging on a Sunday morning when I passed a church just adjacent to my townhouse. When I passed the open doors of the church, I was overwhelmed with the beauty of the choral group practicing in the sanctuary.

. . . .

I COULD NOT KEEP JOGGING. The whole situation captured me, and I could not walk away. I stopped and was drawn like a magnet inside the church. I sat at the back and was immediately engulfed in an ocean of tears. I dropped my head out of fear that someone would see me, and then gradually I pushed myself forward and knelt on the kneeling bench.

Breathing just a little easier, I heard myself saying, "My Father, Oh my Father, forgive"...and was shocked out of my mind when I heard the words I was saying. I could not believe my own words or my action—-that I was actually in a church..., praying and even kneeling and saying, of all things...this was not me at all...that I was sorry...sorry for what...everything or nothing...I had no idea...

Then I found myself standing up and moving across the room looking for someone, somebody, anybody, anything, What the heck...I did not know what in the world I was doing... no idea...except wondering if I was...losing it... and going crazy.

And then as if it were pre-arranged??? I bumped into this guy in a black robe of some kind and a funny little hat. He looked at me as if he knew me and said, "Hello, may I help you?"

I said, "Please, do you have a minute?"

Then to my great relief, I heard this creature say, "I have all the time in the world," as he sat down on a bench and signaled for me to sit by him.

Very carefully, I sat down, not having any idea what I was getting myself into. To my complete surprise, he bowed his head for just a minute and then reached to shake my hand. He said, "Go ahead and tell me the entire story I have plenty of time."

I was completely surprised to find myself relaxed and at ease. In fact, I could have gone to sleep right there. But I resisted the urge, turned to him, and said, "You won't believe this, and I hate to be taking your time, but the strangest thing just happened to me."

This person turned to me and smiled as he said, "If you tell me something I haven't heard before, you get the prize, please proceed." Again, he smiled and bowed his head.

I began talking rapidly saying, " I was jogging, running by that open door and all of a sudden, I was compelled to come in and listen and some kind of explosion happened in my chest. I have never, in my whole life, had a similar experience."

The man turned, held my hand, and said, "I have heard that story many times, please continue. This is a work of God in your life, please continue."

I protested, "But I don't even know God. I don't even know who this person is, that you are talking about."

He turned and looked me straight in the eyes and said, "But He knows you.

"He knows you.

"He knows you.

"Thank Him and be grateful. He finally found you. Where have you been hiding? For a while God was here on the earth in the form of a man—-his name was Jesus of Nazareth. He went back to heaven to be with his Father and sent a Spirit... his Spirit... to do his work after He left. His Spirit is the person who is dealing with you now—- we call Him 'The Holy Spirit.'"

I was frozen in place. I could not think. I could not talk... I could not focus. I could not move...I was totally paralyzed. I sat there and looked at that man a minute and wanted to jump up and run out of the church and could not move, even one finger. Time vanished or stood still or something, I was not sure what had happened, but in my life...—-bigger than anything I had ever experienced.

I gradually began to feel just a little more normal and was able to breathe normally. I looked at this man I was talking with, and he looked normal (except for the funny hat.)

I had an experience of being cold in my running shorts and T-shirt and turned to apologize to this man sitting beside me. He waved off my apology and then asked if I would be more comfortable in his office. I accepted very quickly, welcoming the thought of a little privacy.

I gradually began to feel a little more "normal" though I was not sure, at this time, what that was. I explained to this man, whose name I had learned was "Father Reagan." I told him that I wanted to go and put on some other clothes. He assured me that it did not matter unless I would feel more comfortable.

I went back to my room with my brain almost screaming at me, asking what in the world I was doing or thinking and having no understanding, all I could do was laugh. I laughed and laughed and laughed until I fell on my bed and to my complete surprise found myself fast asleep.

I do not know how long I slept, but it seemed like forever, when I awakened and headed for the shower. With the water pouring down my body, I was mentally going through all the things that I had experienced trying to find understanding and reasons. I did not find any but kept searching.

"Who is this God and why is he messing with my life?" The whole experience was a mystery to me "Is there really a God or just an imaginary concept that people believe in because they have heard it for years?" The questions kept coming without any answers. I thought, "I need to go and talk to Father Reagan again. If anyone knows about this God business, he should." I walked straight to the church and asked for him. A young lady in the office said she would get him, so I found a chair and waited.

He came very quickly and took me to his office. He asked if I would like a cup of coffee, which I gladly accepted. He was very slow and deliberate, which I really appreciated, because I was in no mood to be hurried about anything.

He sat down in a chair next to mine, leaned back slowly looked at me and smiled very slightly, as he said, "My new friend, I want to make one thing clear, before we start. I will tell you what I know, and I will make every effort to be clear and succinct. Secondly, I do not, understand God and what He does and does not do. I don't understand God, I don't even understand myself. I will be glad to tell you what I know, and I will count on your questions to help with my understanding."

I slapped him on the shoulder and said, "Sounds like a winner to me." Then I said, "Suppose I start at the beginning?" He nodded and I continued, "I think I just became a man, or an adult." And I recounted all the things that had happened at home until I had moved into the townhouse next to the church.

He listened intently with no sign that he was in a hurry. Then I recounted, step by step, everything that happened in the church. At this point he stopped me and asked, "Has anything like this or similar ever happened to you before?"

I said, "Nothing ever, nothing ever even close."

He was silent just a moment and bowed his head. I waited briefly and he continued. "My friend, it looks and sounds as if God is speaking and has a message directly for you."

I was shocked at his response and said, "But why?"

He leaned back slightly in his seat as he said, "I told you in the beginning I could not explain God and this is clearly his work," and with this, he looked out of the window.

I was speechless. I sat there and replayed his words in my brain. "What on earth? Was this man telling me that God was addressing me personally, as a man? ...How in the world?... Could he believe and expect me to believe that God, the Sovereign ruler of universe... was talking to me... it... was more than... my brain could ...???"

I stood up; I sat down; I stood up again; then I turned and looked out the window. I had no idea what I should do, say, think, or feel. So, I continued to stay where I was and kept standing.

If I accepted what was happening as real ...and I had no other choice, except to tell myself that I was hallucinating...the truth was I had no other choice...the truth was... it was really true...and I had to deal with reality. I turned and looked at Father Reagan and said, "It is true. It is true. It is true, somehow, some way, for some reason,...God has intervened in my life."

I breathed deeply and fully for the first time in a long time. I breathed deeply and it felt great. I turned and looked at Father Reagan and we both started laughing uproariously.

It was true.

It was true.

It was true.

Father Reagan said, "Man, you are blessed. God obviously has his hand on you. Thank God. Praise God! Praise God!" Then he said, "Would you mind sharing this with a few others?"

I thought, "Might as well—-it's good news. Why not share the good news?" We walked a little way to the other side of the church; he opened a door and I saw several men all robed like Father Reagan.

Father Reagan said, "My brothers, this is our new brother who would like to share an experience with you."

He sat down and motioned for me to stand. I stood and was surprised to hear myself saying, "My Brothers in Christ. I need to first say, 'I have no idea what happened to me and could never begin to say why...it happened... except to say, with a certainty I have never known in my life, that God began to speak with me yesterday without any warning. I was simply walking down the street by the church and heard the music. I was compelled beyond my will to come into the building. Something happened on my insides I cannot begin to explain. It felt like an explosion inside my chest. I took a seat there in a pew and could not move."

Everyone in the room began to smile. There was a whisper of laughter, a lot of, "Thank God, Praise God," and everyone in the room stood in line to hug me and kiss me on the cheek. My heart, mind and spirit soared to heights of feeling I had never known before. As everyone seated themselves, a holy silence filled the room, and I was forced on my knees to pray. A message shattered the doubt and silence in my heart, and I heard a voice, distinct, loud, and clear saying, "It is true. You are called. Do not be afraid. I am with you. You are my Son."

I could no longer kneel. I was compelled to stand, and raise my arms in praise to say, "Thank you, God...Thank you, God...Thank you, God."

CHAPTER THREE

• • • •

I TOOK MY LEAVE AND went back to my room and called my parents. I told them I needed to come and talk with them. They were both glad I was coming, and Mom said she would have dinner ready soon.

We were seated at the table, and I began. "I do not expect you to understand what I am going to say because I do not understand myself, everything that has happened to me in the past several hours."

Mother immediately teared up and said, "Tell me that you are alright." When I assured her that I was well, she calmed down.

Then, starting with the moment I entered the church to hear the music, I told them in detail everything I could think of. They both listened to every word. When I finished, neither parent said a word. We all three were silent for several seconds. I finally said, "I guess you are as surprised as much as I was, so I have no explanation except to tell you, as I did, exactly what happened as I remember it.

My father asked, "Have you ever had any of these feelings before?"

I said, "Never." And I looked at my mom, "Except once, Mother, when I was very small you took me to mass, and I never forgot that moment. Other than that,... nothing."

My father said, "Well, maybe I should have been going also." Then, he added, "How does this impact your contract with Edison?"

I had to answer, "Dad, I had not thought about that one second."

Dad said, "Well, when you have time, you might want to give it some thought." Then, he smiled, and I was greatly relieved because it seemed that I had his approval, which was very important to me.

Mother had gone to the kitchen and returned when she asked, "Does this mean you will be Catholic?"

I said, "Mother, I have no idea, not one until I have some time to think about it. And I plan to do just that——think about this for a long time. Dad, I am sure I will need your input as well as Mom's."

My father said, "First, I think you should talk to Edison."

I agreed quickly, and said, 'Maybe, I need to go now."

But Dad said, "Not until you have eaten!" and we all laughed and began to eat.

I looked at the clock and said, "Edison's offices are all closed now so I guess I will go in the morning."

"What are you going to say to the folks at Edison?" asked my father.

Quickly, I said, "I will tell them the truth. I have nothing else that I can say." My father smiled and bowed his head and continued to eat. Mother got really busy in the kitchen, and I thought she was probably crying.

The meal ended and my father and I left to find seats on the porch.

Without looking at me, Dad said, "Six years of chemistry and you are walking away from all of it?"

I stood up and said, "I do not see myself walking away from anything, but rather I see myself walking toward the biggest and richest adventure of my entire life."

"Great way to look at it, Son. Glad you see it that way. I too, need just a little while to digest this and then I will be able to see it with more clarity." Dad got up and walked over to hug me.

I was thinking about Edison and Mr. Rogers, the senior vice president, with whom I had talked several times. First thing the next morning, I went to his office and asked if we could have a personal and private conversation.

He said, "Of course" and immediately got up and closed the door. Then he dismissed his secretary. He offered me a chair, but I told him I would rather stand. He sat down at his desk, filled a pipe, and began puffing.

I started by saying, "This is very hard for me to talk about, so I will just dive in. I will be telling you some things that I will not be able to explain, and I ask for your patience."

He removed his pipe and said, "Of course, please proceed."

I began, with some difficulty and said very slowly, "Yesterday, I was walking by the church next door to my house, and all of a sudden, I had a very strange and wonderful experience. There was no warning, just very strong emotion on my inside. I finally found someone to talk with when I entered the church. It was a "Father Reagan." He helped me to understand that this was an act of God, which I had trouble believing, but had no other explanation. The reason I am here is to let you know I can no longer fill my contract with Edison." Then, I took a chair and sat down.

Mr. Rogers walked around his desk and shook my hand as he said, "I want to thank you and congratulate you on your candor and straightforward honesty. I wish we had more men like you in the company. I congratulate you, Sir, on who you are and what you are doing. I know Father Reagan very well and am glad you have made his acquaintance."

For me, this was a tremendous boost to my self-confidence and conviction. I thanked Mr. Rogers for several minutes before I left his office. I walked on air for a good distance as I was leaving Edison and going, of all places, back to school. I did not know any other place to go. I knocked on Professor Mullins's door and heard a cheery "Come in."

I walked in and said, "Well, I have burned my bridges and now I am deciding which way to go."

He laughed and said, "Someday you will look back on this and think of it as the most important day of your life. My friend, when I was a child I heard a hymn when I went to a Black church with the man who was mowing grass in my yard. I did not understand the meaning.

I was totally surprised when this man, a Ph. D. chemistry professor, began to sing very quietly,

> *"You got to walk...this lonesome valley,*
> *you gotta walk it by yo'self,*
> *ain't nobody else can walk it fer you.*
> *Yes, yes, yes...you gotta walk it by yo'self."*

Then he said, "I have never forgotten that moment. It was like they were singing it to me and for me. And, my friend, with the path you have chosen, there will be times you will walk that same lonesome road. Be prepared."

I sat down in a chair by the window, overwhelmed and feeling just like I had the day before sitting in the church. God spoke to me then and was still speaking. I had a new feeling, that I did not understand. For lack of understanding, I, in my thinking, called it "THE HOLY."

Later that afternoon, I called Father Reagan to ask about training for the priesthood and he gave me a phone number. I hung up and dialed the number immediately. Of course, it was busy, so I waited and waited and continued to wait. Several more waiting periods and I called again, and the phone actually rang. Some man answered and I said, "I would like some information about entering and studying for the priesthood." I was put on hold, waited, waited, and waited.

Finally, someone picked up the phone and asked me to please hang up. I did, not knowing what else to do. I was determined not to be discouraged in the beginning so, I found a chair, partially broken, and sat down. It was raining and I watched the people come in and shake their coats and take off their overshoes. I did not know people actually wore those things unless they were really old.

I suddenly remembered a Protestant Seminary on the same side of town where I was. Not knowing any name, I could not call. I waited and waited while several people came up and used the phone and watched the rain forever and it seemed like never rather than forever.

Finally, finally, after forever I got to the phone again and asked for a phone number for the Protestant School nearby. I got the number but decided to wait a little while before I called.

Before someone else took the phone I called the first number I had been given. It was busy so I decided not to call and called the number or the Protestant School that I had been given. I dialed and got the message that the number was not a "working number anymore." I was really getting tired of the phones and decided to go home. Mother answered and said supper was ready and I went over immediately.

Driving home, I realized that I was a little discouraged because I could not talk to anyone at either school, but then I told myself that everyone was just as busy, or more, than I was. I could not expect anything from anybody who had no idea who I was and what I was doing—-no one except these two people looking across the table at me right now. This realization seemed to help a little but not much when I was in the presence of Mom and Dad.

I spent the night at home. The next morning, I got busy with Google and found some answers before I started walking the streets. I felt as if I was wandering in an open field of some kind. All of a sudden, I stopped myself, leaned against a nearby building, and talking to myself, I said, "Holdup, right here, Decide what to do then do it—-you are a super-intelligent human being, now stop, decide and then move ahead."

I immediately went to a Seminary which I had passed many times; then I went in the first building I found with an open door. I asked the first person I met where to find the administrative office and went straight there. I went to the nearest desk and asked to speak to someone about admission as a first- year student. I was given a chair, and someone called my name in a short while. I followed the person to the office and had a seat in front of the desk.

The person at the desk introduced himself as Dr. Rollins followed by, "So glad you are here, and I get to talk with you. How can I be of help?"

I responded very carefully, "Sir, I have a very long story and I am not sure you have the time to listen."

He chuckled just a minute and said, "I have all the time in the world and would like nothing better than to hear your story. Please begin."

I took a deep breath and began with my personal story of growing up and the Edison deal and my experience in the church. He never batted an eye and listened intently to every word. Several times he stopped me and asked questions for clarity.

I do not know how long I talked but it must have been hours. The office staff had left and turned out the lights before I finished. I stood, a little embarrassed that I had talked so long and began to apologize, but he stopped me and came around the desk and asked me to kneel so we could pray. I had a feeling similar to the one I had experienced in the church.

So, I knelt down and said, "Thank you, Dr. Rollins. And thank you, God."

He prayed for me and then said, "I want to thank you for this time and assure you that it has been a blessing to me. Please return to the office tomorrow and we will take care of the paperwork."

I left, feeling like I was walking in the clouds. The time with Dr. Rollins was a validation of everything I had experienced in the last several days. Inside, my heart was bursting with a song.

I went back to my apartment and realized that I needed to terminate with Edison and let the apartment go. I started immediately thinking about a place to live, not even realizing, of course, that the school would certainly have housing.

The following day, I went to the school and soon I was assigned a room and glad to have a place to sit down. I then went back to my car and brought all my junk upstairs. I looked at my schedule, the classes I would have, and textbooks I would need; so, I decided to go to the bookstore and shop for a while. A cute little blonde with long, beautiful hair was shopping in the same aisle. She was trying to reach a book on the top shelf. Of course, I offered my help and got a very quick, "Oh, thank you!" and we started a conversation, which led to my asking "Would you like a drink of some kind?"

Her "Yes" was quick... more like an invitation and we found a table for a delightful visit. We were both, "first timers" on the campus and made friends very quickly. I was thoroughly enjoying the visit until I turned around a corner, looked up, and she was gone.

I was shocked. She was nowhere to be found. I looked and looked, then thought, "Well, so much for that deal." I paid for my books and went back to my room. I laughed when I rehearsed our meeting. I didn't have long to laugh because when I got to my room, Hans, my new roommate, was there, moving in. I offered to shake hands when he said, "I am German and speak very little English."

I laughed loudly and gave him a high five. Then I said, "Well, my English is not the best in the world; so, we are both in trouble." He laughed as if he understood. I said, "Bitte gehen con mego" and Hans laughed. But I was trying his language.

The next day Hans and I were walking to the bookstore, and in the middle of the campus, we met the blonde who had run away from me previously. Hans spoke to her in German. She blushed and her face turned a vivid red. Then she said something to Hans who laughed and looked at me. The best I could discern, he was trying to tell me her name was Gretel and something about the reason she left so suddenly last night. While Hans was trying to explain she took my hand and shook it. I was a little amused because the whole situation seemed a little bit surreal, but I decided to lean back and enjoy the picture.

All three of us eventually began to look at books in the shelves surrounding us. There was very little conversation but a lot of smiles and laughter. Some way we did communicate that when any person talked, they would first interpret and then make a statement. There was a lot of laughter and a lot of fun after we began the process. Hans proved to be quite a wit and we both enjoyed him.

It was soon mealtime and we left for the dining hall. Of course, we sat together and each of us described the dishes in his own language. We each were surprised at the few similarities and the differences. When the meal ended each of us went to our own rooms for the end of the day. It was study time which no one doubted.

Several days passed and the language barrier grew smaller and smaller. It soon became apparent to me that Hans had feelings for Gretel that were very romantic. Consequently, I spent less time with the two of them. I was relieved because the relationship had become a little heavy for me. I spent more time studying and thinking about spiritual matters, which was what had brought me to seminary. In fact, I almost became a recluse. I made excellent grades and at the end of the year two professors had offered me assistantships. I was very encouraged, of course, and maybe a little flattered, but there was no one to share the good news.

I knew then that I needed to spend more time interacting with the other students. It was hard at first because I found myself a little bored with the meaningless conversations we all engaged in, at least until I stumbled into a group meeting late one afternoon in the library. I met them when I dropped an armload of books trying to get down from a small step ladder at the end of a table. I fell, not just a little, but I took a really big spill, and when I struggled to get up, I found I had broken my arm.

Two of the guys at the table came to my rescue very quickly. One named Samuel stayed with me in the emergency room until I was taken to surgery. Of, course, I was handicapped to some degree, but before I was released from the hospital I was visited by the German professor that taught my class. He asked if I would be willing to help him teach a summer German class for six weeks. I discussed it with my new friend,

Samuel, who had spent a lot of time with me in the hospital. Then I told Professor Tolar, I would be glad to help him teach the course.

With a lot of physical therapy my arm began to heal nicely. One day I was shocked to see Gretel sitting in my class. When we finished, I told her how glad I was to see her and asked her to have dinner with me. Hans had not mentioned her in quite a while, but it did not occur to me that the relationship had ended.

We went to dinner together and as soon as I got back to my room, I talked to Hans and told him I had had dinner with Gretchen. He was furious with me. He left the room and stayed gone for hours. He came back very late and would not speak to me. I decided it would be a suitable time for me to spend a night at home and visit my parents. I drove home, and, of course, both my parents were thrilled to see me. It was a good time, and I shared a lot about my schoolwork. They were overjoyed to hear that I was helping to teach a summer session. It felt good to be at home for a while.

The next day, I had no classwork and decided to go by the admissions office and talk with Dr. Rollins. I told him the whole story about Hans, and he suggested I go back and apologize again and ask forgiveness. I took his advice and went back. Before I went to the room, I sat in the car and prayed that God would soften Hans's heart so that he would forgive me.

It did not happen. Before I had finished my apology Hans had stormed out of the room and slammed the door. I followed him, simply because I did not know what else to do, and I kept trying to talk with him. He persistently refused to talk, and then I screamed at him, "I prayed that you would forgive me, and you are not doing it. Does God not answer prayer? I guess that is true. There is no god, and no one answers when you pray. I will never pray again."

Hans turned quickly and said, "Wait, Wait, Rob, God answers prayer. I was just being disobedient and not doing what God was telling me to do. Now you must forgive me. I am sorry now. Maybe we can pray together."

Before I knew it, Hans was on his knees. I knelt down. There was nothing else to do. I put my hands on his shoulders and asked God to forgive and to bless us both. I opened my eyes and looked at Hans and saw his eyes full of tears. We both laughed and said, "Thank God." It was a good and holy moment for two people who were trusting in God.

We were both quiet for a brief time and then Hans jumped in bed and said,

"I am going to take a nap." So, I decided to do the same thing. It was several hours before we were both awake and I heard Hans get up.

His first words were, "I feel better now."

I said the same thing and we shook hands and said, "Let's go to lunch," and we were on the way. We were both back in the room and reading, in about an hour. Hans said, "I want to apologize again for my bad behavior."

I said, "Once is enough. Let's move on," and that was enough. The misunderstanding was over.

After a few minutes, Hans said, "I think I will go and apologize to Gretel and tell her how wrong I was and that I am sorry."

"Great idea, man. Let me know how it goes." As soon as I said that, he was out the door. I was so very happy to see how quickly he made the change.

I needed to go to the bookstore; so, I took off as soon as Hans left. It was late in the afternoon and the sun was barely visible in the West. A girl caught up with me and said, "I'm Marie. Mind if I walk with you? This is not my favorite time of day. I am not a night person. I love the daylight and the sunshine."

I turned to her and said, "Well, we make a good team. I am the opposite. I love the night." She chuckled softly and said, "Can't imagine that. The dark has always scared me." We both laughed a moment and walked in the door of the bookstore.

I looked at the girl and thought, "She's a good looker." So, I said, "Can I buy you something to drink?"

She said, "I would love that." We found a table and I ordered two malts, and we exchanged names. (She was Marie, from Michigan.) She asked, "How did you know I wanted a malt?"

I said, "Oh, I am a mind reader. In fact, that is one of the courses I am taking this semester—Mind Reading 101. Have you ever tried it? Go ahead right now and read my mind right now. It is easy."

She hit me on the shoulder and said, "Crazy man. But I do know what you are thinking—-You were going to ask me for a date tonight."

I said, "Bingo! You nailed it. That is amazing. You are a natural, but I am having a little trouble right now. So, what was your answer?"

She hit me gently on the shoulder again, "I can't get ahead of you. You are too quick."

I said, "You are right there, and I work to keep my speed. I am fast on my feet."

She looked away, "Don't need any mind reading here. That is obvious." We were quiet for just a minute.

I asked, "Are you a senior?"

She answered, "No, junior and one more year. Will be glad to finish."

I asked, "What profession do you plan to pursue?"

"Teaching I guess, I really haven't prepared for a career and earning a salary."

"Then, get married and let your husband earn the salary." I just thought I would play with the idea.

She was quiet for a moment and said, "That is one option. But it might be too expensive.

I responded, "Well, you have lots of choices, that's for sure."

She looked at me and said, "You married?"

I said, "No, not old enough. I guess."

Her laughter was free and easy as we continued to walk across the campus, and she suddenly said, "Goodnight, enjoyed the visit."

I said, "Same here" and we went our separate ways.

As she walked away , I wanted to call her back and felt that I was not finished with the conversation. So, I turned around and ran to her and told her exactly what I was feeling and thinking. She laughed heartily and almost screamed, "I was feeling the same thing." Then she kissed me on both of my cheeks, and I loved it.

I said, "Crazy girl, this is more than a drop by casual acquaintance. So, you tell me about you, and then, I will do the same."

"You go first," was her very quick response.

I laughed and said "OK, Thirty years old. Just started seminary training as a new Christian. One younger sister. parents live here in town. I am a very good skier and a better student and plan to finish school in one year. Your turn.

She paused momentarily and said, "We might have a problem with this 'new Christian' thing. I have had some bad experiences with that sort of thing. One of my sorority sisters has been trying to convert me for a full year."

I was ready for her response and said, "We both have a past, so let's make a deal. I won't be responsible for your past, and you won't be responsible for mine."

She immediately said, "Great idea. That will work." And she threw her arms around me and said, "So we start as friends, no problems."

We walked to my car, and I said, "Could we go for a ride and talk. You can drive, if you would like."

She jumped in the driver's seat, and we took off. She drove very slowly, and I said, "Recently, I have had two major experiences, and I would like to tell you about both. If it gets too heavy just tell me, and I will stop."

She looked the other way and said, "Would you please drive?" So, we changed places and I said, "Marie, I will be glad to tell you, but I do not think I can explain why it's happened."

She said, "No apologies, just keep talking."

So, starting with the major step of personal growth, I told all the details. She listened and said, "That scares me to death, thinking that I may need to do the same thing."

"Do not worry. If you really need it...It will come to you," was my response. She listened very attentively, and I was impressed. I said, "This is the person you are talking to. No frills, just me. Then I went silent just to see what she would say.

"Sounds to me like an adventure for both of us." I gave her a high five and she said, "One thing is – it won't be boring."

I responded, "You are right there, my friend. I cannot imagine you being boring."

She leaned over and kissed me on the lips, and I leaned over and held her in my arms for a full minute or more.

I sat back for a minute and said, "Marie, we have to slow down because I am just out of a broken relationship and I am not sure of my feelings—not even a little bit and I cannot allow myself to be dishonest with you, even though we have just met.

She laughed for several minutes and said, "I don't— I don't, believe it because I was a just going to say the exact same words to you. Did you read my mind again? I was shocked when you started and almost asked you to stop for fear you would think me dishonest when I talked. In fact, I would like you to meet Chip. He is a senior and finishing early this semester, come on, I want you to meet him, he is in the Student Center, I just saw him there."

Crazy, I know, but here I was going with a stranger to meet her "ex" not knowing either one. We laughed and both said, "This is crazy" and kept doing the crazy thing. She walked up to this guy and said, "Chip, this is my new boyfriend."

This guy stuck out his hand. We shook and he said, "Good luck to both of you." He looked at Marie and then me, and said, "She is a great gal." He slapped me on the shoulder and said, " Sorry, I've got a class and have to run. Good luck to both of you."

And, with that he was gone. I suggested we get something to drink, and she was ready, so we sat and talked briefly until she said, "Am I going to get to meet your ex?"

I said, 'I really don't know. I think she went home for the weekend, but I really would like you to meet her. Maybe later." I had some reservations about her meeting this girl I had just told goodbye. It seemed very strange to be meeting the exes, but I just decided to play along with the game even though I was not sure what "the game" was.

We walked out on the campus and then over to her dorm. Another girl was coming out dressed in her tennis outfit and she looked beautiful. Marie stopped her and said, "I want you to meet someone. We were thinking about dating each other." She rolled her eyes, shrugged her shoulders, and said "Good luck! Flirts with everything and anything wearing a skirt. Can't stand him. Gotta go. G'bye."

Without any other word she was gone, and I stood there looking at Marie. I said, "She may be right. I was reared with a bunch of girls, and I call it 'play.' My kid sister insists I am a flirt." Then I said, "Why don't we have dinner and see how it goes. Sounds crazy, I know, but what the heck. I'll buy dinner. It is worth the price."

We had a delightful meal and laughed a lot. I said, "Marie, do you think we might try a date or two, with the agreement that each of us is free to leave any time we choose without explanation. We were both laughing (as much from relief as anything) but we had a delightful meal. (I was surprised) I said, "If I didn't know you quite so well, I think I would ask for a date."

She laughed, heartily, as she said, "And you know, I might even consider saying 'Yes. Isn't that strange? OK, then, just to experiment, please, a trial, but I warn you, I am hard to please."

"Join the club, me too, was the response." We had decided to go dancing and she looked stunning in her outfit. I was really overwhelmed for the first few minutes. The guys all lined up to dance with her. I found myself feeling proud she had come as my date.

When we got to her dorm, I did not kiss her goodnight, though I could tell she was expecting it. I waited a moment just to see what would happen. She said nothing but hurried in the door and left me on the steps.

I did not call for the next several days. I waited, hoping she would call. She did not. I waited several days and asked her to go with me to a fraternity function, but she said, "I am sorry, but I have other plans. She came with one of the campus football heroes, I tried to keep out of sight, but I bumped into her on the dance floor and had to smile and say, "Sorry."

I watched her on the dance floor. Obviously, she was the most popular and without a doubt most beautiful. I decided not to call— too much competition. This was a very familiar position for me. When competition arose, I dropped out always and always. Did not see myself as an adequate competitor with the star of the football field.

Then, one day, she called. I had trouble believing it was her and asked, very awkwardly, what she wanted. She said, "Well, stupid, first I wanted to know why you stopped calling me."

I was trapped and I knew it. I could not think of one single thing to say except to tell the truth and I was not ready to do that. I was quiet. Until I heard her say. "Gotcha, and I am not going to listen to any answer until you are looking into my eyes when you speak." Without another word I heard the phone hangup. I stood frozen for a moment and could not move.

Crazy. The next night was "Date night" on the campus. My phone rang and it was the hostess saying, "A lady in the lobby is waiting for you." I dressed in nothing flat and ran down three flights of stairs, burst into the lobby, and saw this magnificently beautiful human being sitting across the lobby smiling and waving at me. I went over, took her hand, and said, "I have something to say to your eyes...that...

She said, "Wait just a minute for the tears to clear," so I took her, and started the dance that I knew would last a lifetime.

Difficult to Find
CHAPTER ONE

· · · ·

ROB JUST KEPT WORKING, changing tires, and tightening lug nuts. He did this knowing that all his schoolmates were at a party where he could or should have been invited. But he was working in his father's garage "on the wrong side of the tracks" (small town society term), as the saying goes. Everyone knew what it meant, but no one liked it.

He knew and had been told that "side of town" was where he lived, which was the reason he understood was why he was not invited to all the parties with his classmates. It hurt, of course, to be snubbed by all those who could be friends. But...he kept working (and helping his father) as best he could.

No one knew or recognized, this young man had a fire burning in his insides that refused to be extinguished. On his insides, it sounded like this: "Someday they will beg to come to my house—across the tracks or wherever."

He was preparing for success in whatever field he chose to enter. He promised himself, "In everything, anything I do, I will be the best—the best student, the best athlete, in anything or everything, I will be the very best—-with no exceptions." He graduated, and was not the valedictorian but promised himself, "When I finish college or graduate school, I will be at the very top. I promise myself. I promise God. —-nothing less than the very best."

He never forgot his promise to himself or his promise to God.

He finished all his work and went to his father and asked if anything else needed to be done. His father laughed and said, "That is all. Let's go home."

They walked, both laughing, hand in hand across the railroad and down the street.

Rob bounded up the steps and into the house, saying, "Mom. I am starved."

His mother Kathleen said, quietly, "You always are, my dear." And both men made it to the table.

"My dear, you need to tell Rob, the news you got today," Kathleen said.

Rob's dad dropped his head just a little and said, "Well, you didn't make it to Harvard, but Princeton said, "Come on and hurry."

"You are in, my son! We have sold everything we could and mortgaged the rest. I have borrowed every penny anyone will lend me."

Rob went to his mother, then to his father and hugged them both. He said, "There is no way I can thank you so I will just do that by being the best student in the entire school.

His parents both smiled and said, "Just do your best and that is enough for us."

Rob stopped and said, "Could we pray right now?"

Robert Sr. bowed his head and said, "Father, you gave us this young man at birth. Since then, we have tried to be good caregivers; so, we constantly give him back to you. We pray in the name of Jesus. Amen."

Meals in Rob's home had always been happy times mostly because his mother had always been very happy. Rob could not afford to be any other way.

Rob went to his room immediately after the meal and found the book he had been reading. Every night he was reading the classics and had been doing that his entire life. It was part of his daily schedule, reading until midnight and sometimes later.

It was 5 a.m. Rob's light was on, and he was reading, as was usual for him every morning. His mother came in with a cup of coffee and a muffin. Rob's mother was "a great gal" and he loved and always enjoyed her.

At eight o'clock the next day he was back at the garage helping his father. The two of them sometime worked together, and sometime separately, depending on what jobs needed to be done in the shop. Today, they were working separately all day long.

Rob had responded to a "flat tire" call, several miles from town. As he was returning in the tow truck, he was surprised not to see his father standing in the doorway like he usually was.

He parked the truck in the usual place, crawled out and went inside. Not seeing his father, he was a little alarmed and looked at the cash register. His father's body was on the floor in front of the cash register and Rob could see blood gradually seeping out of his head. He ran to his father's side and turned his body over; he knew in that moment that nothing could be done. Blood was also coming from bullet holes in his chest.

He grabbed the phone and dialed 911, got someone on the phone and asked for an ambulance.

Knowing there was nothing he could do for his father, he jumped in the tow truck and went to get his mother. It was very hard to break the news to her, until they got to the hospital and saw the team of doctors and nurses standing around the ambulance.

Rob put his arms around his mother and held her closely. She was screaming and crying alternately. Rob could only stand with his arms around her.

Several days later there was the funeral. Friends came from everywhere. Rob had to feel sorry for his mom. They were so close, and Rob knew she would miss him. In just a few months, she was doing okay. Rob was surprised when he saw her go right back to functioning more or less normally. He saw a resolve, a determination in his mother he had not seen before.

When Rob stopped and really thought about it, it came to him that he could not leave his mother at home alone and go to college. At first, he was overwhelmed with the realization and then it got a little easier.

He wrote to the admission office at school and explained the situation and why he could not go for the fall session.

He began to keep a journal recording his thoughts and feelings to help him make sense of all the changes in his life.

• • • •

JOURNAL ENTRY #1

I was completely surprised when I received a letter from the school saying that I could enroll, as a student and do all my work at home, as a first-year student working with my computer. I was overwhelmed and wrote a letter of appreciation immediately. By return mail, I received all the information I needed to be enrolled as a full-fledged freshman. Needless to say, I was overwhelmed with gratitude and wrote to the school immediately to tell them.

In a few days, I received all my assignments and my books for my classes. I was more than thrilled and immediately sent a check for my books and tuition.

I received a letter from someone named Mary Alice (Something)saying she would be my correspondent with the school. She gave me her address and phone info and even sent a small photo. I am thrilled to be in direct contact with the school.

• • • •

JOURNAL ENTRY #2

Several weeks have gone by with the new arrangement. I did well on my first three tests sent from the school. In fact, I scored 100 on every test I received in the mail. That feels great and

I continue to read all four of my textbooks and some of them twice. I am keeping the garage open and studying between customers.

The police have come several times and questioned me, and I found out that the people who called about the flat tire were working with the man who shot and killed my dad. It surprised me to know that he was on the FBI's ten most wanted list. He was soon located and killed in a shootout.

• • • •

JOURNAL ENTRY #3

The police came today and brought me a check for $10,000.00, which was the reward for the capture of any person on the ten most wanted list.

I closed the garage and took the check to Mom. I laughed out loud when I heard her say she could not take it because it really belonged to the spouse or family of father's murderer who had been killed by the police. That was so like Mom.

We talked to the police, and they said we should not give it to the murderer's family. In fact, they said, we could not give it to them.

I was very proud of Mom when she said, "It is my money, and I can do whatever I choose to do with the money." After she said this, she went over and kissed the police chief on the cheek. I almost laughed out loud when I saw his face turn red.

Journal Entry #4

We got the address of the family of the man who killed Dad, drove about fifty miles to find his widow. I had a lot of conflicting emotions while we were looking for the house. We drove in the small driveway between two old, abandoned pickups. Mom went to the door with the money(She had cashed the check because it had Robert Morgan, Sr.'s name on it.)

The woman screamed, got down on her knees and pushed the money away. I looked quickly at the condition of the house and the dirty little ragged children playing in the dirt. It was not a pretty picture, but Mom marched straight into the kitchen and left ten piles of one-hundred-dollar bills on the table.

I walked outside because I could not watch another minute. Mom came out and jumped into the car. I said, "Are you finished?"

She said, "Maybe." We drove out of the driveway and started for home.

• • • •

JOURNAL ENTRY #5

Yesterday, we took the money to the murderer's widow— today a strange thing happened. I went in to open the garage, and around noon, this woman showed up, in overalls, and started stacking all the junk around the garage in neat piles. She was cleaning up every little nook and cranny, giving the place a total and completely new look. After she had worked several hours, she came to me and said, "I'm Sadie. Do you have a real cold coke anywhere?"

We both sat down and drank a coke—agreed to be friends forever and then she left walking two miles to her home.

• • • •

JOURNAL ENTRY #6

This morning, when I got to the shop Sadie was there and had painted nearly half of the front of the garage. It looked totally like a different place. She walked over to me, put a twenty-dollar bill in my hand and said, "Go to Walmart, I need more paint."

I went without asking one question. I brought it back and she went straight to work. By 5:00 pm she had painted the entire front of the building. Before she left, she told me, "I'll be here every Saturday to work inside while you work outside—-no pay, See you later.

She walked away on her two-mile trip home.

As I finished the day, I stood just before I locked the door, and thanked God for my mother and my new friend, Sadie.

When I got home tonight, I told Mom what had happened

and she said, "Well, thank God! I am so glad. That will free up my Saturdays!"

After dinner I spent a couple of hours reading my textbooks for school. I love the experience of learning new material. I feel myself learning and growing. I can't help remembering that this whole new experience of life started with a tragedy. It is more than I can comprehend but I laugh as I remembered the

*rapid unfolding of events that have taken place in such a short
time.*

After reality began to set in for Rob and Kathleen, they had dinner each night, mostly in silence, as they reflected on all the things that had occurred since Robert, Sr.'s death. One night Kathleen said she had some things she needed to take to her new friend Sadie, and in a few minutes, she was gone.

Rob watched a football game briefly, on TV and then went to his room to read.

When his mother had not returned, he began to get a little worried. He went back to the garage, got the tow truck, and drove to Sadie's house. When he pulled up in front of the house, he saw Kathleen and Sadie sitting on the porch. There was a man on the floor with his hands tied behind his back. Rob jumped out of the truck and ran to the porch. Kathleen pointed to the man and said, "He made a little mistake and tried to rape me. I grabbed him in his privates and pulled real hard (That was what my daddy told me to do if I ever had trouble with a man.) He was more than glad to back away. Sadie was standing on the porch and quickly came with an axe to help me."

Kathleen and Sadie were both laughing and Sadie said, "He will never try that again!"

Rob sat down by the man tied with ropes and said, "That was my mother you were trying to rape. Be glad you didn't make it because if you had, I would have skinned you and put you in that fire."

Kathleen came over and said to Rob, "I think he wants to help you in the garage tomorrow."

"Yes, Ma'am, I would be glad to do that." was the anxious man's quick reply.

Without another word he jumped in the back of the tow truck and sat down. Rob started the truck and took off going back to the garage.

As soon as the truck stopped at the garage, the man jumped out and stood nervously still. Rob reached out to shake hands with him and asked his name. He dropped his head and softly said, "Willie."

It was late, but Rob asked, "Willie, would you like a coke?" Willie did not answer and acted as if he thought he was going to be hit or shot. Rob said, "Well, I will see you tomorrow, Willie," and Willie just stood there. "You can go now."

The puzzled man walked away very slowly looking back every one or two steps like he did not know which way to go or what to do. Rob called out, "Come by tomorrow, and we will talk." After a pause, Rob said, "Goodnight," but got no answer.

Rob went home, mentally and physically exhausted, while he reviewed the events of the day. Though he wanted to enter the night's experience in his journal, on this night, his bed was too inviting; he jumped into bed immediately and was sound asleep.

The next day when he got to the garage, Willie was standing at the door waiting. Robert spoke to Willie very quietly, "We are going to work together to see if you want to be my friend or go to prison. The Sheriff will be here in a little while to talk with you. Please don't get scared and try to run away, because I have already posted bond for you and hired a lawyer. Just have a seat here a wait a little while."

It was nearly an hour before the sheriff arrived and Willie looked as if he was going to jump out of his skin. Marshal Dillon (not the TV character), came and brought cokes for all three of them, took a chair and moved over by Willie. It was funny watching this scene. The Marshall began to explain,

"I am not here to arrest you. Robert, here, has asked that we hold the arrest to see if you had rather work or go to prison. We will let you decide. I will stop by often to see how you are doing. As long as you are working and pleasing Robert, you will stay here and work. He will also pay you a salary. I would appreciate it if you would see me and Robert as friends and not as enemies. Do right and work hard and you have nothing to worry about. Step out of line, and I will shoot you or put your butt in jail. You have a choice that I have never seen given to a man, let's see what you want to do with it." Willie was very quiet for a moment, but Marshal Dillon and Rob heard him say, "Sho' do thank y'all!"

As soon as the marshal left, Willie picked up a broom and started sweeping the back of the garage, which had not been cleaned in years. Rob just watched and let him sweep. Several cars came and went. Willie went to everyone and asked politely, "Can I help you?" Rob was more than pleased with his actions. He dispensed the gas, oil and even cleaned the windshields.

When the day was finished, Willie shyly went to Robert and said, "I am a pretty good welder...making signs and stuff like that there." Rob jumped in the tow truck, waved Willie inside, and went straight to the welding shop. When they were inside, Rob told Willie, "Get what you need." Willie selected a good bit of stuff, more than Rob wanted to pay for, but he thought a minute and decided to take a chance.

Arriving back at the garage, Willie told Rob, "I need several hours to work if you don't mind. I will lock up and walk home when I finish."

That evening, after a couple of days of scary, unusual events and encounters, Rob returned to his writing in his journal.

• • • •

JOURNAL ENTRY #7

I may have made a friend today: Mom was assaulted yesterday...and after she told her assailant he would be helping me in the garage, he came, and I put him to work! Tonight, I am thinking, "Am I losing my mind?" but then, ..."What the heck, might as well take the chance." At the end of the day, I am remembering my father's words, "Son, sometimes you have to trust people even when you feel you are wrong."

When I got in the tow truck and started home this evening, for some reason, that I could not understand, I felt compelled to go to the cemetery where we had so lately buried my father. I opened the gate and walked in and closed the gate behind me. I drove a short distance to the spot where I had buried my father, stopped the truck, got out, and stood there praying. I cried very hard.

All of a sudden, I realized someone was standing by my side. I stepped back just a little, turned just a bit and saw Libby Reynolds, the head cheer leader in our high school who was also elected "most beautiful" in our school. I was in shock and said, "What are you doing here?"

· · · ·

ROB STOPPED WRITING and thought back to that encounter at the cemetery and the exchange that took place.

Libby responded to his question, "Oh Robert, I was out of town, all week, the day of the funeral and I was just passing by when I saw your truck pulling in and I just wanted to stop by and be with you just a minute. I know you must miss him, Robert. You know of course, I never had a father.

"My parents married, and my father went down in a plane two months later, on his way to Europe. Never even knew him enough to even speak to him." Mother never remarried. She dropped her head when she finished and became very quiet.

Rob apologetically replied, "I never knew any of that Libby, I am very sorry, I never asked."

"You never had the chance," she responded and pulled a small weed off the top of the grave. "I have admired you for years, but you never looked at me. Can you tell me why?"

"Little Girl, I never even dreamed you would be interested in talking with me!" She turned and hit Rob hard on the shoulder, stepped back a little, and giggled.

Rob confessed, "I had exactly the same feelings toward you. I wanted to flirt with you but never got close enough for you to notice—so look, I am flirting with you now—-got the message or do I have to draw you a picture? "

She laughed out loud and said, "Got the message." Then he grabbed her and kissed her really hard. She laughed, leaned over, and put her head on his shoulder and did not move.

They both stood there a minute, very still and totally quiet. She stepped back just a little and raised her face to be kissed again. He did kiss her lips, but first, once on each cheek.

Unnoticed by the couple the grounds keeper had stood just across the road. They heard him say, "You two love birds need to be going. It is past six o'clock and I need to lock the gate."

He turned and started to walk away, but then he stopped, very suddenly, turned around and started walking back to them. He took Libby's hand and put a little grass ring on her finger. Then, he said, "I made one of these a long time ago and put it on a little girl's finger. I hope you two will be just as happy as we have been for the last 50 years, and may God bless you both."

They started to the gate and Libby said, "Well, I didn't really expect to get married today but who knows what surprises one day can bring."

Outside the gate they stopped, and Rob said, "Libby, I hope we can have a friendship." Then he took her hands and set them on his lips and said, "Let's dispense with the formalities. I love you, and you know that already. Do you have the same feelings, or do I start kissing you over and over and over and over and, and, and...Well, you get the message?"

He picked her up and held her for a long time, kissing her several times. He did not want to put her down, but he walked over the steps to her car and sat her down. "Go home," he said. "Think about this and we will talk tomorrow,"

She said, "I will dream about you all night like I have been doing for years! I love you, crazy man, I really do and have for a long time, so fasten your seat belt. I am going to be a part of your life." Then she grabbed Rob's face and kissed him again real hard. He thought He was going to faint but got control of himself and helped her into her car.

Rob didn't take the tow truck back to the garage because he wanted to walk home to catch his breath. He made it home and Kathleen was waiting on the porch. He was so excited, he told her every single thing that had happened.

She listened quietly and said, "You won't believe this, but you are talking exactly about the time when your father and I first made a real connection. My first contact with your father was almost identical. I am happy for you both. I found it hard to keep listening when you were talking because it was so near what we had experienced. I am still having trouble believing what you said. I was a crazy impulsive person just like you are describing Libby to be. This has to be a work of God."

Rob was shocked to hear a loud banging on the front door. Kathleen was shocked also and said, "Who in the world can that be?" They both went to the door and there stood Libby.

She burst into tears, grabbed Kathleen, and said, "Oh, Mrs. Morgan, please don't think I am a bad girl because I'm really not. It's just, it's just...Oh I have loved him so long and he would never even look at me. Please, please... please don't think I am a bad girl. I have just been afraid for years that I would lose this man. I went home and told my mother and stepdad and they said, 'For goodness' sake, go and tell them the whole story.'

"Please don't think I am bad. It's just...it's just. ...Oh, I don't know what else to say."

Kathleen stepped forward and grabbed Libby and hugged her as they both dissolved into tears and laughter.

Not knowing what else to do, Rob grabbed them both and hugged them in a big hug.

In just a minute, they heard a knocking at the door, and Rob went there to see Libby's mother standing there waiting. They had a long visit and Libby's mother explained that she had worried because Libby had never been interested in dating anyone.

Of course, she did not know she was waiting for "Robert" to notice her. Robert made a date for breakfast before Libby left.

After spending the better part of an hour, lost in reliving each moment of the experiences of the evening, Rob laid his journal aside and tried to go to sleep. He did not sleep much that night and neither did Libby. They were both early at the restaurant the next morning.

At breakfast, Rob was very anxious when he told her about Willie, but she agreed with everything he had done and said she wanted to meet him. Her response both surprised and pleased Rob. He found it hard to believe she was so quick and willing to forgive. After telling Libby goodbye after breakfast, and as he neared the garage he nearly fell out of the truck.

On the top of the building was a big figure of a huge black bear—-he was really huge and holding up a big sign with cut out letters saying MORGANS' GARAGE and underneath BEST IN THE WEST and underneath in smaller letters " robert and willie." The larger letters were all outlined in small blinking lights. Rob jumped out of the truck and hugged Willie and thanked him over and over. It was an unbelievable moment. The sign looked very professionally done.

Rob had a hard time stopping his laughter. He guessed this made it official: Willie was changing his name from "Rob" to "Robert." His father had always been Robert, but now he owned the garage, and that is the name by which Libby called him, so it was decided!

Robert called the marshal and asked him to come see the new sign. Dillon was just as shocked as Rob was. He went and found Willie to congratulate him. Willie was pleased with all the recognition he was getting.

Willie came to Robert and asked if he had a "coupla minutes to talk." Then he said, "I don't know what you folks plan to do with me; so, I don't understand all this good treatment you are giving me. Hope you are not planning to shoot me when you are through with me."

Rob had him sit down and give him a coke. Then he said, "Willie, my family and I are trying to be Christians and like Jesus said, 'Return good for evil.'"

Willie stood up and said, "Well, I ain't never heard nothing like that in my whole life! Sounds a little crazy! Is that what y'all are trying to do wif me, if'n it is, then I'm gonna be a Christian too...never heard 'er nothin' like that, sounds crazy to me, but I sho' wants to join."

He popped his hand on his overall covered knee and said, "Count me in sho' nuff. I like that game you are playing. Beats anything I ever heard of."

Libby had walked in unnoticed and stood listening near the door. She came over and put her hand on Robert's shoulder and said, "Willie, I am a Christian, also, and we are glad to have you join us."

Willie stood quickly and said, "Sho' do thank you ever one." Libby hugged him, and Rob thought he was going to faint.

He said, " Willie, a few years ago God came to this earth and his name was "Jesus Christ." Not everyone believed he was God's son but all those who chose to believe in him— these are the ones who are called Christians. We will be talking to you more and more about him. When you say you believe in him, he makes a change on your insides which we call, 'being born again.'"

Willie laughed out loud, "That is good news to me. I shore need a new start."

Libby said, "When we talk to him that is what we call prayer. We will be talking with you more about that also."

Willie said, "You mean I can talk with that guy? Hot Dog! sounds great to me. Never even thought about talking with God and not cussin. I don't mean to be impolite, but you two people is a little bit strange." He spoke very quickly and then hurried away. "Well, I got some work to do so I'll be moving on."

Libby looked at Robert and they both smiled. It was then Robert said, "I have to get in contact with school. I haven't even thought about school in two or three weeks. I will call Mary Alice and see what I need to do to catch up."

They talked on the phone, and she brought Robert up to date, after he told her what all had been going on in his life. She was very interested and asked a lot of questions. He tried to answer as briefly as I could. She was very helpful and seemed to be genuinely interested in what Robert was doing.

That night before bed, Robert returned to his journal:

• • • •

JOURNAL ENTRY #8

> *At home tonight, I was completing some of my schoolwork when Libby walked in and took a seat. I was so happy to see her and glad to see her walk in like she felt completely comfortable in my home. Strangely, she seemed instantly comfortable with me as I did with her. I finished my work, and we went walking in the semi-darkness. I felt as if we had known each other and been friends all our life. We talked a lot about school, and she had already enrolled in a nearby teachers' college.*

Much to Rob's surprise Libby went the next day to the business office where he was going to school and told them of an emergency that required her to change from Teachers College and transfer there. The change went through like clockwork and in less than twenty-four hours she was a student with Robert in the same school. She even enrolled in the courses he had signed up for.

• • • •

THAT NEXT NIGHT ROBERT had an exciting entry in his journal:
Journal Entry #9

This morning when I found my chair in physics class, Libby was sitting by me. This woman is a complete mystery to me. She was on my heels every minute, but I certainly did not object to that. I tried to talk with her and send her home, but she would not budge. This woman is a different human being from anyone I have ever known. I am so flattered I cannot stand it.

I have studied very hard and knew the answers to every question asked by the teacher today. Long ago, I made the decision to be the top student in every class. Now that Libby will be by my side and listening it was more important than ever.

• • • •

ROBERT CONTINUED HIS journal now with a focus on his school experiences.

• • • •

JOURNAL ENTRY #10

I am trying to be careful not to be a "know-it-all;" however, when the class was over today, Dr. Sadler asked to talk with me, I was so excited I could hardly contain myself, and Libby was equally excited. The professor first talked about grading papers and then being an assistant instructor in the lab work.

I was thrilled at the thought of being a lab assistant since this position was usually given to seniors. I was being very careful when I said, I am not sure that I am experienced enough to be a lab instructor. He turned away, so I said, "Whatever you decide, Sir." We left the classroom walking on clouds.

We could hardly wait to get to the Student Center to begin to meet the other students and that is what we did for nearly an hour. I felt like a king walking through the Center and introducing myself. Libby was enjoying the time equally with me and had no shortage of guys wanting to meet her.

· · · ·

DURING LUNCHTIME ON the campus, Robert and Libby continued to meet new friends and share stories. One day, Robert had just started their meal when a guy at the table began to ask him questions. He said, "I think you have just recently met a distant cousin of mine. Do you own a garage in Clayville?"

Robert answered, "Yes, Willie and I have become really good friends. He has brought a lot to the business."

The guy choked just a little and said, "Well, I hope so."

Robert decided to let the conversation stop there and went on to something else. No one at the table paid any attention to their table talk, but Libby punched him under the table and said, "Nice going there, guy. You handled that well."

As they left the table, the questioner asked Robert if the two of them could have a cup of coffee. He started the conversation before Robert had said a word. "I know the whole story so we can dispense with all the trivia. What I want to know is: How in the world did you know you could trust Willie? Anybody that I ever knew or heard of would tell you that he is the biggest con man in the U.S."

Robert looked him square in the eye and said, 'Did you ever hear of a man named Jesus Christ?'"

Robert's response caused him actually to reel— Robert almost reached out to catch him. The guy stood and stared at Robert with his mouth half open and both eyes blazing.

"Well, I...of course...I go to church and all that but, Man, what you are talking about is something entirely different...how in the hell did you know you could trust him? What in the...were you thinking...Man. You are crazy! You are something else... I always heard that Christians were crazy but, Man, you take the cake...I never even heard of anyone like you.!"

Robert decided to use both barrels and said, "He is running my shop right now, and has keys to the cash register and the combination to the safe."

The guy abruptly left the conversation and went into the men's room. He stayed a good while before he came out. He came straight to Robert and said, "I am twenty years old and never heard a story like that one time...not one time...,man, you are nuts...you are a damn psychopath,...you are crazy as hell...and now I guess you are going to tell me that you want me to be a Christian. On the other side, I don't give a dam about you being a Christian. That is your business, but don't bother me with it."

Robert was trying to decide what to say or do when Libby walked up and said, "I don't think I have met you, I am Libby. Then she said, "You two guys know each other?" The guy with Robert had been talking could not say a word. He simply turned around and walked away.

Libby said, "What was that all about?"

Robert could only say, "Tell you later, Babe," and they walked away.

Robert took Libby to her dorm and then went to his, thinking about how nice it would be to be married and not have to separate at bedtime. He was beginning to have feelings for her that he had never experienced. He suddenly realized they had not discussed marriage and thought they should do it the next chance they were together.

That following Sunday night Robert wrote in his journal.

. . . .

JOURNAL ENTRY #11

Church with Libby seems different. We went to Early Service today and came back by the garage. We drove up to the front of the building and saw the door closed and locked. I was a little upset; I got out of the car and went to the door and saw a crude hand painted sign on the door that read. "GONE TO CHURCH———COME JOIN ME——OPEN IN ONE HOUR——HURRY BACK—-willie." Libby was standing behind me reading with me and we both burst out laughing.

I am absolutely thrilled at the changes Willie is making on his own and without any coaching from me. Willie drove up at just the same moment and said, "I hope you don't mind; I have been listening to a radio preacher and he said, 'If'n you wuz a Christian you were s'posed to go to church, and I figured I had better start. I hoped you didn't mind."

We laughed together and I suggested that he go with us every Sunday. He said he would get some new clothes and go with us. I thought Libby would never quit laughing from sheer happiness.

After we left the garage, I drove outside the city without lunch and found a neat side road. I got out of the car, came around to Libby's side, got down on my knees and asked her to marry me. She jumped out of the car and into my lap and we both rolled over and over in the dirt. With both of us crying we got up, dusted each other off and I said, "I don't have a ring yet."

She interrupted me and said, "I already have a ring," and showed me the one that the man in the cemetery had put on her finger.

She was still wearing it! I was speechless! She had covered it in plastic so it would not fall apart.

I loved that gal!

We, I guess, I, had to begin to look for a place to live, an apartment or something.

• • • •

THE IDEA HIT ROBERT really hard—-marriage—-He could barely comprehend the thought.

The next time they were together, Robert shared his thoughts with Libby and was glad to know she was having thoughts very similar to his. They were both beginning to think about two persons instead of one—huge change!!!

Robert had saved quite a bit of money to pay for college (not even considering marriage). They sat and talked about finances. In their talk, it became very clear that they needed to have more income. Libby said she would drop out of school and work, and she could get her education later when Robert was working.

He did not like that plan at all and insisted that she get her education first. It seems they had their first disagreement: she was firm and even insistent that Robert finish school first and she should go to work and support both of them. The discussion was not resolved, not even before they went to their separate dorms. It dawned on Robert during the night that his assistantship paid his tuition for one semester.

He hadn't even considered that. In the middle of the night, she called and woke him up, reminding him of that. They laughed a long time before they hung up and both went back to sleep.

The next Sunday in Church, there was an announcement made that the Church was looking for a new Director for Youth Activities. Robert was thrilled to put in his application for this job. He was not optimistic because he knew so few people in the church group. He and Libby waited several weeks without hearing, and had pretty much given up hope, when Robert got a call asking him to come in for an interview. They seemed to be ready to offer him the job. Since Robert had the possibility of this new position it meant that both he and Libby might be able to attend classes together. They waited and prayed.

One day Willie asked Robert if he could talk to him alone. Robert found time, and they went to the back of the garage. He told Robert that he was learning to read and write and had found a book called "First Reader" in a car he was working on. He said that he had been visiting Sadie and she was helping him learn to read and had even practiced writing his name.

Then, Willie told Robert he wanted a Bible, "If you don't mind."

Robert told Libby, and she immediately went to the bookstore, bought a beautiful leatherbound Bible and had his name put on the cover. He was totally overcome when they gave it to him and asked where to start reading. They told him to start at the book of John and explained about the four gospels. His gratitude was so great Robert and Libby were embarrassed. He told them that he listened to a certain radio preacher every night.

Robert made good progress in his studies and his grades were at the very top in every class. His work with the youth group at the church cut into his study time but not too much. He found that his self-confidence was improving. Libby, of course, was a big help and worked right by his side.

They had been married little more than a year when Libby began to have stomach problems. She got up every morning nauseated and could no longer prepare breakfast. They eventually decided to go and see her doctor who told them very quickly that she was pregnant.

They were shocked and thrilled at the same time. They laughed and planned for several days. Then they began to talk about the expense of a new family member in their home. It seemed scary and bittersweet first, until they decided to trust God and be excited.

Robert made a Journal Entry in his journal that night.

. . . .

JOURNAL ENTRY #12

Libby and I looked at each other tonight as we were going to bed, and I said, "God has always been with us, and we are going . . to believe that this baby is simply part of his plan. So, we are going to trust Him and be happy." We are thrilled beyond words and can't wait to tell our parents and friends.

After that things were much better, and Robert and Libby were thrilled at the thought of a new son or daughter in our home.

. . . .

THE BABY CHANGED THE world for them, even though they had not seen a face. Libby took on some sort of glow and developed a beauty she had not previously displayed. Students would stop her on the campus just to tell her how beautiful she was. Robert felt he was married to a movie star. She claimed her beauty and seemed to enjoy it almost as much as she was enjoying the pregnancy.

Other students on the campus began to talk about "our baby" and the parents-to-be became celebrities almost overnight. There was a lot of laughter surrounding the entire pregnancy experience. Classwork continued as usual and seemed to take priority over the baby and everything else.

Robert was surprised with Willie's behavior. He started wearing white overalls every day with the Garage name on the back. The garage began to make more money than it had in years. In fact, it started making money every week and it had been a long time since the garage had made a profit.

Robert raised Willie's salary as the profits increased. One day at the end of a very profitable week, Robert asked the sheriff to come and talk with him, Libby, and Willie. We made an agreement that would allow Willie to continue to work there and buy the garage with payments each week. Willie was absolutely exhilarated! They all congratulated him and got a huge bottle of coke to celebrate the occasion.

After the celebration Willie asked Libby and Robert to come to a back room in the garage and said, "Sadie and me gotten kinda close since she been teachin' me to write, 'n spell and all that."

He asked if that was alright, and, of course, Libby and Robert agreed. When they went back to the front Sadie and all five of her children were there. Willie said they had found a house near the garage and rented it. He said, " She is making money cleanin' houses and we are getting sorta rich because we have more than two thousand dollars in the bank right now."

Willie said, " Now, Mr. Robert, I ain't taken nothing from the garage. You can look yo' self 'cause every penny is right there, I promise. You and the sheriff can count every penny."

The Morgans had become very pleased with the way things were going with Libby's pregnancy, Robert's job at the college, and Willie and the garage. One evening, Robert heard the front doorbell ringing.

Robert could not imagine who would be showing up at the door at 10:00 pm, but he went to the door and found Willie standing there.

Willie was half talking, and half crying and he finally got out the message that Sadie had gone to the doctor's office that afternoon and the doctor said she was going to have to have some surgery that would cost thousands of dollars. Willie was saying he would just take her back to her house in the country because "I didn't know she was in that kinda shape when I started fooling with her. And if she is in that kinda shape she will just have to take care of it herself because she didn't tell about this when I asked her to come and live with me."

He did not like it and kept saying he wanted to take her and the kids back home. Robert even explained that if one of the kids got sick it was his responsibility. He strongly resisted that thought and it took several more hours before The Morgans could convince him. Finally, after several more hours of talking and explaining. He began to understand, but he did not like the idea. When Robert asked him, "What would happen if you got sick, what would you do?"

Willie became totally silent and dropped his head when he said, "I ain't never thought about that. Guess I would jess have to die like a dog in the bushes."

That is when Robert said, "Willie, that is what we are trying to tell you. We don't live like dogs; we live like humans caring for each other and loving each other. Now get in the car and we will go and take your wife to the doctor, and you will tell the doctor you will always be there to help and protect your wife."

He got in the car and dropped his head and held it with both hands. Robert leaned over and said, "Willie have I ever lied to you?"

He looked up and said, "No, Sir."

"Well, I am not lying now so go ahead and do what I tell you to do."

Willie very quietly whispered, "Yes, Sir." and said nothing more.

In the car on the way home, they continued their discussion, and it seemed Willie was beginning to understand.

The next morning, Willie went to the bank and brought back two thousand dollars. Robert explained that he could pay a little each month and not the whole bill at once, so Willie went back to the bank with his money. Robert made arrangements for the hospital to diminish the total and give Willie a monthly payment plan. He was so relieved, he burst into tears.

Libby was very proud of what Robert was doing for Willie and the family. The next day they were told that the hospital arranged for all the children to attend daycare facilities. The college got wind of what the Morgans were doing for Willie and his family and paid half of the balance due on the bill. They were thrilled to get the news.

The next morning Willie was at the garage and Libby and Robert were on their way back to college. Libby picked up Willie and bought flowers and took him to the hospital to see his wife who had just returned to her room after surgery.

Amazingly, the children were perfectly behaved in the day care facility. Libby said she thought they were scared to move.

A couple of nights later, Robert had a phone call from Willie, and he was yelling, "Help me. Please, help me..!"

Robert jumped in the tow truck, called the sheriff, and drove as fast as straight to the garage. Willie was in the garage with the door locked, and there were three guys trying to break open the doors to get in. Of course, when the men saw the sheriff drive up with flashing lights, they all vanished immediately.

Willie explained, "I didn't owe them nuthin'! We wuz gambling a long time ago, and I caught them a cheating on me, and I left the game."

The sheriff laughed and said, "The next time they show up, call me quick." Things settled down and everyone went home.

That semester, Robert got the top score in the physics class and Libby did the same thing. Robert was a little peeved, but Libby said, "Tuff, my friend, I will beat you next semester."

Robert grabbed her and gently kissed her, "Go for it, Gal."

Things seemed to settle down quickly, Sadie was making great progress after her surgery. Willie brought flowers faithfully and told everyone he could about how well he was taking care of his wife. The children stayed in hospital childcare for a few days, got all their shots and lots of new clothes. Willie went to the head of the hospital to thank everyone and asked if they could stay a few more days. The hospital authorities said "No," quickly. Libby made arrangements for the kids to go to a state sponsored kindergarten. The change in their behavior was dramatic.

Dr. Wright, The professor of Robert's physics class, asked if he would like to be lab supervisor for the Senior Class. Robert was stunned when he heard the question and was told that his stipend would double and would pay his tuition and Libby's. The semester went amazingly well and Dr. Wright made arrangements for Robert to take an aptitude test in physics. Again, he scored at the top and was granted full scholarships for both him and Libby.

Dr. Wright asked them to come to his office. He told them that he had offers for them to attend graduate school but only one scholarship. Robert looked quickly at his wife's extended stomach and had no trouble declining the offer. When they left the room Libby insisted that he take the scholarships and leave her there. His answer was clear, "Not in a million years." They stayed another year on college campus to welcome the most beautiful, happy, bouncing daughter in the whole wide world.

Of course, both of their mothers were there, and the baby daughter received a royal big welcome.

But beyond anyone's comprehension or understanding tragedy struck.

One morning when the baby was only a few weeks old, they went to the baby's bed, she did not move or respond. Of course, there were the 911 calls and the calls to doctors and mothers. he only response they received was IDS. (Infant Death Syndrome) no explanation and no understanding. (The name was later changed to Sudden Infant Death Syndrome SIDS.) That was the only diagnosis for a death that no one could explain or understand.

At first, Libby was hysterical and frantic, Robert held her as she held the lifeless daughter and no one else heard when he said, "You still have me and I still have you, please don't forget."

Libby fainted and gradually slipped to the floor. Robert picked her up and helped her to a chair. One by one the people began to leave. Robert got down on his knees in front of Libby and said, "I know of only one thing to say to you or myself. In the presence of death, always look at what is left, not at what is lost."

Robert stood again, not having a choice or knowing what else to do until he felt Libby's body relax and lean a little harder on him. Her mother came over and asked if they could sit down at the table, whether or not they ate. They had been seated just a minute when someone came and whispered that Willie was there and wanted to speak to Robert.

Robert went to the door and there stood Willie dressed in a coat and tie and Sadie standing by his side. She had on the shabbiest dress Robert had ever seen. She walked over to Libby, "I want to kiss you." She was holding a small package in her hand.

Libby grabbed them and kissed both of them. Then she brought both of them into the dining room and had them sit with her.

Libby then turned to Willie and said, "Will you pray with us?"

Willie bowed his head and said, "Mister God. I don't know you very well, but I'd just like to ask you one thing. Would you please take this little girl which we can't keep no more, and jus' hold her in your arms till we all gits there to live in yo' house and we would sho' be much obliged to you. I guess that's all I wuz going to ask you, Sir. and I sho' do thank you fer letten me talk to you jist a minute. That's all, Sir."

Libby stood up facing everyone in the room and said, "I just want all of you to know, I have given my baby to God, and I trust Him to take care of my baby until we all get there to be with Him. "All the people who were there stood and sang "Amazing Grace."

Libby and Robert walked home beneath the light of a beautiful silver moon, with their arms around each other and went to bed thanking God for friendships." The funeral, next day, was a celebration and everyone left the cemetery celebrating a loving God, who was holding the precious baby in his arms.

· · · ·

THAT NIGHT WHEN ALL was quiet, Robert took comfort in writing in his journal for the first time in a long time.

Journal Entry#13

I am surprised at myself when I find myself comforted as I picture God holding my child. Libby has had a harder time and has said two or three times that she wants to go and be with our child. At times like this we both try to picture God holding our baby. Then we could actually picture God holding our baby in his arms.

· · · ·

LIBBY AND ROBERT ACTUALLY laughed several times remembering Willie's prayer. Robert's mother was overcome but looking to the future. Time began its healing, but time heals very slowly.

Robert and Libby were both thinking about being back in school and wanted to be there. The necessity of reading and study changed their focus and soon they were deeply involved with school.

CHAPTER TWO

....

SEVERAL YEARS PASSED almost without their notice and they found themselves back in school every year Robert had good grants and scholarships which took care of their tuition.

They talked at length about post graduate study but found it hard to make a decision on that subject. They finally decided to go ahead with their graduate studies, without further discussion about another child. Then, they found that Libby was pregnant. They were both overjoyed and did not ever talk about the child they had lost.

Willie told Robert he wanted to buy the garage and Robert was glad to sell it to him. Libby's mother moved into the same city to be near her only child. It was almost time for the Morgans' second child to be born, and everyone but the two of them were getting anxious. Their studies still consumed a major portion of their time, so before they knew it Libby went to the hospital for the delivery of their second child.

The delivery took place perfectly. In a few days, the family was on the way home. The new baby was home, happy and healthy, and everyone breathed a sigh of relief.

Libby chose to do her work in chemistry, but Robert chose philosophy. Their only problem was that there seemed to be a personality conflict between Robert and Dr. Hughes, the head of the Department of Philosophy. This was more of a problem because Dr. Hughes had to give final approval to Robert's dissertation before he received his degree. Robert asked for a conference with Dr. Hughes and the request was refused. Robert re-sent his request—this time, the request was approved.

Several days later in a class, the professor made this statement , "I want to be crystal-clear on this point. In my opinion, there is no supreme being, there is no god. These words are only ghosts from the childhood of an ignorant parent trying to get a child to go to sleep. The book that the Christians call the Bible is a collection of fairy tales and anecdotes."

Robert immediately stood and said, " Professor, would you please tell us a source or an authority for your statement."

The room grew suddenly very silent when Dr. Hughes leaned over his desk and smiled just a little. He immediately said to Robert, "Evidently you have a different opinion. Would you mind telling me and the class exactly what your objection is to my statement."

Robert paused just a minute and said, "Professor, you have taught us–this very class–always to require the other person in a discussion to prove his point. Is that what you are doing with me right now? With all due respect, Sir, I refuse to answer your question for the reason you yourself have taught me in this classroom."

Dr. Hughes burst out laughing and said, "Touché, my friend, good thinking. Now that you are dueling with your sword—-"THRUST."

Robert stayed very calm and said, "PARRY."

Dr. Hughes sat down at his desk and said, "Robert, you are doing a great job. Please proceed."

Robert did not falter and said, "Please tell me one book older and with more history than the Bible authenticated by several codices, primarily *Sinaiticus,Codex Vaticanus*, and others. Name me one other book so fed by the blood of martyrs as is the Bible.

"And one thing more, Dr. Hughes, name just one other book, just one that has been received and embraced as the billion copies of the Bible distributed around this world in more than three thousand languages and dialects."

Dr. Hughes sat at his desk smiled and said, "My friend, I congratulate you whole-heartedly on being informed so well on this topic of discussion and the way you presented your material. Again, I congratulate you whole -heartedly.

"One more thing, my friend, I would like to challenge you to a debate in the Student Center on a Saturday night at 9:00 pm."

Robert said, "My dear and revered Professor, I accept your invitation with gratitude."

Libby was shocked and overwhelmed. She had trouble believing that Robert would debate a professor. She watched him skim through a few books and asked if he was going to study more for the debate. He told Libby that before he had left home his pastor had spent an entire afternoon telling him all he needed to know about the Bible and its history. Libby was shocked and still a little afraid, but she decided to trust her husband.

Saturday finally came when Robert and Libby arrived at the Student Center just a little late. The room was packed with students with some standing in the aisles and doorways. Robert went straight to the rostrum and shook hands with the professor. He went over to his desk and bowed his head to pray for just a minute.

Dr. Hughes stood and welcomed all the students and thanked them for coming. He introduced Robert and had Libby stand in the audience. He then introduced himself and had his wife and children stand in the audience. The applause was very heavy when he was seated.

He asked one of the students to come forward, write the numbers one and two on slips of paper and drop them in a hat. The student complied. Robert dipped in and drew the slip numbered two. He bowed to Dr. Hughes and sat down.

Dr. Hughes stood and gracefully thanked all the students for coming. He recognized his wife and children again. Then he said how much he admired Robert and appreciated having him in his classes and as an assistant.

He began his presentation, "I was reared in a Christian home. My mother and father were very faithful members of a local church. Every

Sunday without fail, our family filled our favorite pew, dressed in our Sunday best. I had nothing but love and respect for my mother and father and the God they believed in. The same was true of my three brothers and two sisters. My parents believed and lived the Christian way of life. A change took place in my thinking and feeling sometime in my twenties.

"I read for the first time that the date written in my Bible (not really a part of the Bible) was not accurate. I was told that God had written the Bible and there were no errors. As a youth, I received no new information or instruction. I do not remember any significant information as a teenager or young adult." Here he turned and looked at Robert. and he said, " Do you think I am wining the debate for you?"

Robert leaned back in his chair, laughed, and said, "I will take all the help I can get."

Dr. Hughes continued, "Can you imagine what happened in my brain when I am casually trolling through the library at the University and see, out of the corner of my eye, a book with the words, *God Is Dead* on the cover? I grabbed the book like a lifesaver, someone had just thrown a drowning man, opened it quickly and saw the word 'Perspectivism.' Before I could turn a page, I was reading, 'To live is to suffer, to survive is to find meaning in suffering.'

"I dropped the book and walked out of the building and into a fog that did not clear for several days. I went to my room and sat on my bed. I could not think. I would not allow myself to feel anything. My whole world had just fallen in a tumbled heap of ashes. I lay back on my bed and said to the father in my head, 'Did you lie to me? Did you ever read Nietzsche?'

"Furthermore, more reading told me that this great (?) man rejected morality, a concept on which my faith was based. He also rejected any belief in afterlife."

Robert leaned back in his chair, laughed, and said, "I will take all the help I can get."

Dr Hughes continued, "When I am casually trolling through the books here and see on out the corner of my eye, A book out of the corner of my eye, I am always interested and want to be the first to read it and boast to my friends. But when Barth, and the 0thers were doing their thing, Bultman and the others were not doing research, they were pontificating theologians but professors in an argument.

"For example, the majors codexes are not even mentioned.

"It seems to me that the major sources for the book they were quoting would at least have been mentioned. Or maybe one or two anyway, it seems that *Codex Siniaticus* and *Codex Vaticanus* are the two most popular or at least the two most quoted. Of course, age isn't everything but it would seem that the age of these documents would carry some weight when we place value on the earliest documents in man's search for knowledge. I claim no exact dates, but I believe they would both date sometime early in this century."

Robert began, "On the contrary, my honorable professor, I am surprised that Barth, Bultman, and their kin never even mention these writings. I have serious questions as to why they didn't and I am forced to question when they did not make any mention, and not wonder if there is a contradiction here.

I yield the floor to my honorable professor..."

The professor bowed his head and consulted with his colleague. There was a moment of bombastic silence when the entire room was quiet. Not a sound was heard in the meeting.

It was then that Robert spoke up and said, "I would like to recommend that we have a break in our discussion until this same time next week. I offer that as a motion. The motion carried immediately and the meeting began to dissolve.

Trip to Somewhere

It was not possible and yet it was happening to me. Incredible, unbelievable and yet I could see, feel, and understand everything that was happening. I had just left my job, as postal clerk in the city post office where I had been employed for years.

I had walked out the door at the end of my shift. Instead of the familiar surroundings that greeted me at the end of my everyday activity—-everything was strange. The familiar sights, sounds and places that I knew so well were all gone. I stood motionless and tried to get my bearings. Realizing I had totally lost myself, puzzled, confused, and overwhelmed, I was faced with a world totally strange and a world where I recognized nothing familiar. I made a wise decision to stand totally still. For safety, I moved over and stood against a tall black pole with a light shining brightly from the top. Trying to regulate my breathing I leaned hard against the pole and closed my eyes. The noise of people passing brought little comfort to me.

Finally, in desperation I reached out and caught the sleeve of a passerby. The man obviously startled, turned to me, and walked quickly away. I heard myself, saying, "Will you please call a policeman for me?" I asked another person and got the same response. The next stranger paused, just a moment, turned and walked away without replying or looking back.

I was obviously puzzled and had no idea what to do. I decided, in desperation, to sit down on the sidewalk. I sat down and pulled my knees up close and sat very still and waited. It seemed forever but finally I felt someone tapping against the sole of my shoe. I looked up and found myself staring into the face of a policewoman. To my surprise, she was smiling and said, "Had too much to drink, Lad?"

At her request, I found my ID, handed it to her and tried to explain what had happened. The policewoman looked puzzled but seemed to understand and called an ambulance. In a short time, I was loaded onto a stretcher and put inside. There was an attendant, and he was trying to explain. She stopped me and began to take my blood pressure. I decided to relax and be quiet and strangely I was asleep in just a few minutes.

I woke up aware that I was being taken out of the ambulance and into a building. Again, I tried to talk with the attendants but saw quickly that no one was listening. Again, I decided to be quiet, nothing else was working. After being wheeled into a very large room with a lot of very bright lights, I sat up and hung my legs over the side of the stretcher. An attendant came quickly, asked me to lie down, and strapped me to the stretcher. I cooperated and lay very still.

A nurse came with some kind of pad and began asking questions. I tried to answer but found he was very confused and had trouble understanding her or the questions. She left and another person, apparently a doctor, came and began asking questions. Again, I was having difficulty understanding and answering the questions. Finally, I remembered checking out from work. I reached in my pocket and showed them my slip dismissing me from work.

The doctor looked at the slip, came back and began more observation. Not knowing what to do I lay very still and waited and waited...and waited. The doctor this time had an entirely new set of questions. Still having difficulty understanding I tried my best to understand and answer coherently.

I heard clearly, "What is your name?"

I answered clearly, "Marc Thomas." I took out my driver's license and showed it the doctor. More questions, this time quite different. "Have you taken any new medication, any drugs, have you drunk anything, new and different?" I smiled and answered, "No," then watched the doctor walk away.

I was beginning to get worried as I became aware of what was happening in the emergency room. Strange, I was asleep again before I knew it. Sometime later, I was awake and aware that there were people standing beside my bed. Again, the questions started, "Is there a history of mental illness in your family?" Have you ever heard the words, "Alzheimer's, in your home?"

I did not answer. I just lay there and did nothing.

After more delay, a young woman wearing a doctor's coat came to my bed and smiled, and said, "Well, Marc you have quite a situation. How in the world did you manage to do that? I am a psychiatrist and I have never talked with anyone who is dealing with the same thing as you are. Thank you for letting me talk with you. Now, will you start and from the beginning tell me exactly how this happened." She smiled and tapped me on the shoulder, and I felt comfortable as I started talking.

"I really don't have a lot to tell. I work at the post office sorting mail, eight hours a week.—been doing that for years. Went to bed last night. Slept soundly as far as I know. Came to work, rode the bus, worked eight hours, punched the clock, checked out and walked to the corner. That is all, everything that I know... Except–except–except...all of a sudden, I realized that I did not know who I was or where I was going...I did not even remember where I had been—nothing about work or the day. I did try to reach out for help, but no one would respond. I vaguely remembered my name.

"I did not know what to do and no one would stop. So, I just decided to sit down until someone noticed me and stopped. I am lost. I guess...sort of...I know...never been... like this in my whole life. I want to go home but I don't know what I will do when I get there. Do you think you can help me?...Can I be helped? Am I crazy? Are you going to discharge me? What is going to happen next?"

She smiled, took my hand, stood there for a minute, and checked my pulse again. I could do nothing but lie still and wait for something, nothing, anything, Then I heard her say, "Well, it is said 'A good night's sleep never hurt anyone,' so I think that is the first thing we will do. I am going to give you something to help you sleep, and I will see you in the morning. Don't go away and I will see you tomorrow." Then she stuck a needle in my arm, and I was gone for the night.

I awakened in a state of absolute terror. Did not know what to do or say so I lay perfectly still and waited for something to happen. I did not know what I was waiting for or if I was waiting for anything. Finally, finally,...finally, a nurse came to my bed and took my hand to check my pulse. She stood for a minute and said nothing. Then she took my blood pressure and disappeared.

I had no idea what was happening, so I lay still and closed my eyes. I had never felt so lost and alone in my entire life. I gritted my teeth and was determined not to panic, even though it took every ounce of self-control that I had. I realized I was in deep trouble and did my best to stay completely still. I did not know what to do or say, so I was very quiet.

A brief time passed, and the psychiatrist came to stop by my bed and said, "We are going to try something just to see if it helps. We will only do this if you are willing. We are going to take you to your workplace in the post office just to see if that sparks any memories." I was more than glad to give it a try.

The next day, two attendants came and helped me to get into a wheelchair and we rode in a van to the post office. I was unloaded and helped to go in the handicapped entrance. Strange, I felt perfectly comfortable in the familiar setting of my workplace. I actually laughed out loud. The nurses with me held my hands and watched me carefully. I was so glad to tell them that I was aware and knew where I was. We gradually moved back to the ambulance that I had come in, and I sat and talked with the nurses like my old self. I laughed a lot on my way back to the hospital and felt very normal as far as I could tell.

We came back to the same bed, and I began to talk to the doctor whose name I found out was Dr. Markum. I was happy to tell her of my new discovery. She congratulated me and said that I had done everything, except we needed to find out the cause of the problem I had the previous night. I was so glad to be free of the problem, and I did not want to waste time looking back. We moved to her office, and she began an unlimited number of questions——some I could answer and some I could not. She stopped after a half hour, came over and sat in a chair beside me, and said, "I am going to talk to you personally for a while—no longer doctor-patient."

I was very interested especially when she said, "I have a child who is handicapped, much like you have been. I was wondering if you would be interested in helping me as I try to parent this young man and come to live in my home." I will pay you well, and we can talk about that." I was very interested, as we talked about salary and other necessary concerns.

I was discharged and went back to my apartment and spent the night without any trouble. The next day, Dr. Markum and I had another very long conversation about working together. I found out her husband had died in a plane crash several years earlier. Her son. Robert was very easy to relate to, and I was happy to have a new and different job. I asked Dr. Markum to talk with me one night. There were medical ramifications, about which I knew nothing, of course, and I made a request to sit in on Robert's next medical evaluation. It was approved and I was glad to sit in and hear all the medical news. In the first session, I listened carefully but gave no input. I listened intently for two hours but learned nothing of significant importance.

I moved my gear to her residence and became just a little more comfortable living in the home of another person. We decided that I should call her by her first name, Marie, instead of Dr. Markum.

After about a month, we had all settled down to our new living conditions and life became fairly stable. Marie was beaming and happy most of the time. I was very comfortable with my relationship with Robert. He seemed to accept me very quickly and I was grateful for that.

When Marie and I shopped for groceries together, which was a new experience for me, I did a lot of learning very quickly. We laughed and played together in the grocery store like two children. I learned very soon that this "Doctor" had a beautiful child on her inside. I did not learn a lot about her family of origin except that both parents were deceased and were killed in an auto accident at the same time. She had no siblings. My family was much the same and our union was very simple.

I was not really clear about our relationship. She sort of acted like I thought a sister would, even though I never had one. There was no sex. We each respected the other's privacy. It was several days before we discovered that we were almost the same age. She was just a few years older than me. I laughed when I discovered that.

She went to work at the hospital every day, and I took Robert through his daily regimen. We made arrangements so that I would be gone every weekend to give both Robert and me a break from each other. One of the problems was that Robert would not talk. I began to work with that on my very first day with him and was amazed at his response. He was happy trying to learn and we laughed a lot while he was beginning to make sounds. Of course, his mother was overjoyed.

Several months passed very swiftly and I found, much to my dismay, that I was getting bored. I talked with Marie and told her I did not know how much longer I could keep up the pace. I was surprised when she broke down and began to sob.

We talked for a long time one evening, and she said she had started having feelings of affection for me. I had not entertained any feelings like that because I considered her so far above me—-socially. She was a professional and I was a postal clerk. The conversation changed rapidly when she jumped in my lap and kissed me soundly. I was totally and completely shocked but then she continued the kissing and of course, I responded.

That was the first night we slept together and had sex.

Then the next morning, Robert pushed the bedroom door open and stood there clapping his hands and said-very clearly three times, "Hooray, hooray, hooray" There was nothing to do but laugh, which we did and got up and hugged him.

Marie did not go to work for several weeks and we made plans to marry. I insisted that we have a prenup which she and her lawyer worked out. There was no time or opportunity for honeymoon, so we decided to play and have fun at home. We did that, and I had never experienced happiness the way the two of us did in the early days of marriage. It was an actual state of bliss for both of us. Neither of us had expected to move toward marriage. Marie and I both were happily surprised.

Marie and her attorney arranged her finances so that I got a regular income, and it was a great arrangement. I ran the home, took care of all the food and was responsible for Robert day and night. We worked out a schedule that gave each of us free time. I had never thought of marriage and never dreamed it could be so wonderful.

Finally, it was time for her to go back to work. This required a new schedule at home, which Robert and I worked out very quickly. Some days she took the bus and left the car so I could teach this young man to drive. Surprisingly, as he learned to drive his talking improved. This was an amazing and unexpected moment for all three of us. Robert was more thrilled than any of us.

For some reason that we never knew or understood, Robert began watching religious broadcasts on TV. One Sunday, he suddenly announced, "I am going to church." We were both totally shocked but he dressed himself, in his coat and tie and stood by the door until we were ready. When we got in the car, he told us the address and, shocked and stunned, we drove to that very address.

Once in church we noticed he opened the hymnal but did not try to sing. He kept the hymnal open at the right place but did not sing. On the way home as we were all quiet, we heard, the words, "The preacher on TV told me I could talk, and I could sing." Marie and I were both too shocked to reply or say one word. In the silence, that ensued, Robert said, "I plan to talk and sing every day."

Marie burst into sobs and buried her face in her hands. We drove home in total silence. It was a sacred and sober time. When we walked in the house, Robert went in the kitchen and for the first time in his life said, "I am going to make some coffee."

Marie disappeared into the bedroom. I followed and found her on the floor as she said, "I cannot believe all this is happening. It is not possible."

I suggested we call the pastor of the church, which we did, and he came over immediately. He was not surprised at what had happened and said he had received many calls of people being healed in and near the church. Robert was attracted to him instantly. The visit went well, and the conversation flowed freely. The pastor invited Robert down to look through the entire church building and explore the organ if he was interested. The next day, Robert called the pastor very early and made arrangements to come especially while the organist was practicing. He visited the church and met the organist. When he returned he went straight to his room and did not say a word to anyone.

Marie went to his room and found him lying across the bed with a pillow over his head. She sat on the side of the bed and waited for a few minutes. Robert got up, stood by the side of the bed, looked past his mother, and said, "I am going to learn to play the organ and I take my first lesson next Monday." Marie was speechless, said nothing, got up, went out on the porch, and cried for a very long time.

We were both completely overwhelmed with all the changes taking place with Robert. Later that week, we went to the hospital and had a session with the speech therapist. He replied, immediately, "Do not change one single thing, let him make every decision he can and will make. Give him room and expect miracles." We could not believe we were getting that kind of response and obeyed all the instructions verbatim.

Marie came in and talked with me and said that all the changes taking place were largely due to me. I quickly gave the credit to God because I knew I had had nothing to do with all the wonderful changes taking place in the life of this young man. It was nothing less than a miracle worked by the hands of God. We both went back and talked with the pastor of the church. He was very humble and gave all the credit to God and thanked us for coming. We were overwhelmed with gratitude.

When we were talking to the pastor, Robert disappeared, and we looked and looked until we found him visiting with the janitor and helping clean the carpet. The changes in Robert were dramatic and spectacular. We had many conferences with the pastor. He said, "Accept the changes. Thank God and congratulate Robert." We did exactly that. because we did not know anything else to do. Marie took Robert to a specialist and got no new information except, "a slow maturation process."

I gradually became aware that my life had taken a dramatic turn for good, after what I thought was a major tragedy. I laughed out loud when I realized the truth in that statement. I had no choice. I had to believe that somewhere a merciful and benevolent God was looking after me. This led me to believe in Jesus Christ as the true Son of God and the Saviour of mankind.

I had a sense of presence that was new and unfamiliar. It was almost, but not, like someone was holding my hand or my heart. I became aware that I had been a loner all my life. Being reared without my parents had caused me to learn to be independent from the first time that I had any memories of any kind. This new feeling I had was very strange but not uncomfortable.

The organ lessons were a delightful experience and Robert was ready each day when it came time for him to practice. I had secured permission for him to practice on the church organ and he found time to practice each day. Once in a while, the pastor came and listened while he practiced. This made Robert a little nervous at first, but he became accustomed to it. The lessons continued and Robert's skill at the organ continued to increase.

His mother seemed to be happy beyond words. She worked regularly at the hospital and seemed to be happy with her schedule. Marie and I gradually became more comfortable with each other with the passage of time. I was thrilled with this and then time took on a different meaning.

Marie was home from the hospital every day at 5:30 pm. On rare occasions when she was late, she always called to let me know. On this particular day, I kept waiting for her to walk in at a few minutes past five. She did not come and did not call. I began to worry and called her regular number. Her supervisor told me that she had left at the usual time. After the call, I waited and waited for what seemed like an eternity. Finally, I could stand it no longer, so I called the police.

An officer whom I had met several months earlier answered my call, but said he did not have that information.. I was glad to talk with someone I knew, and he said, "Yes, there had been an accident at the hospital between an automobile and a garbage truck."

I asked about casualties, and he said he did not have that information and I knew he was not telling the truth. I jumped in the car and drove straight to the hospital. Robert was asleep so I did not disturb him. The journey was quick, and the policeman met me at the door. I knew when I saw his face that it was bad news. He offered me a chair and a cup of coffee. I could hardly breathe.

Finally, he said, he had called the chaplain who was going with me to the morgue. I do not remember anything except walking behind the policeman. We went into a large room, and he pulled out a container from the wall. I felt a rush of cold air. I knew what was happening and got down on my knees to embrace a small cold frame that I knew was once my wife. I could not rise and everyone left except the chaplain, so I stayed there and held her cold lifeless body for a very long time.

After some time, the chaplain touched me on the shoulder and asked if I wanted to stand up. I did not want to let go. I wanted to stay there and hold on to whatever was left of life in Marie. Not knowing what else to do I followed the chaplain into the next room. Someone brought coffee, but I could not move my hands to pick it up.

I turned to the policeman and asked, "Can you tell me what happened?"

He dropped his head and said, "The truck driver was inebriated. He is incarcerated now. He backed into her and through the windshield. You can talk with him later if you wish but not now. I stood in some kind of fog or smoke and for a minute could not move. The policeman said, "I am going to drive you home, someone will bring your car later." Without thinking I walked out the door and to his car. I got in the car and waited for the policeman—-

It was then, much to my surprise, I heard myself talking—even if I was not sure it was me. I heard, "If you don't mind, I would like to talk with the driver of the truck." Without a word, he turned around and drove to the police station.

We stopped in a reserved space, and I followed him to the cell blocks in the back of the building. Without explanation, the policeman said, "Arthur this is the husband of the woman you just killed."

The man, exceptionally tall, dropped to his knees and said, "Go ahead and kill me. I ain't no damn good and never have been. Take his gun and shoot me. I don't want to live no way. Oh my God, 'cept there ain't no god. Go ahead and shoot me. I don't care. I sho' don't want nobody to be forgivin' me. I can't live after I done something like this...oh my God, oh my God, but there ain't no God. Please for God's sake shoot me now."

Without thinking, without breathing, without any thought, I walked up to the man and put my arms around him and heard someone (maybe me) saying, "Don't worry, I forgive you and God told me to tell you that he forgives you, too. It's OK man. It's all right. Everything is all right."

He fell to his knees and then lay flat on the floor. I heard him saying, "I can't stand that. I had rather die than be forgiven." The chaplain looked at me and said, "If you don't mind, I would like to handle this, and you can wait outside."

I waited outside for what seemed to me a very long time and then the two of them came out. Arthur was smiling as he shook my hand and did not want to let go. He dropped my hand and put both arms around me. I felt like I had run into a grizzly bear. When he let go, I noticed tears in his eyes. I gave him my name and address and invited him to come and see me.

When I was finally back at home, though I did not know how I got there or who took me, I went into the bedroom and lay down on the bed. I got up immediately but did not know why. It was almost like lying on the bed was a denial of something, though I did not know what. I was uncomfortable in my own skin but did not know how, when, or why. I finally decided to make a cup of coffee even though I did not want anything to drink except it felt kind of normal to make a cup of coffee.

My wife was dead. We were planning her funeral. I hated the thought and waited for someone to tell me it was not true. No one came with that message. The silence in my house was deafening and I could hardly stand the burden of the silence. It was like a weight on my shoulders, or my heart, I could not tell which place. She was dead. She was dead. She was dead. I walked outside and checked the mailbox—-nothing there.

Relieved, I guess. No feelings. Funny thing. I always had feelings, but not right now, but the feelings were there, I did not really care that no feelings were there. ————

The funeral director told me that Arthur had asked to speak just a few minutes at the funeral service. Time came for the service. Arthur stood and after a very long silence said, "I want you to know, I am responsible for Marie's death. I was drunk, driving a truck and hit her car—-her husband Marc forgave me. The chaplain said, 'Just like God forgives us.' I don't understand nothin' about this, but I decided to believe him, and I want you to know I have been forgiven—didn't deserve it, but the chaplain said I didn't have to. (In fact, he said, I probably couldn't understand it.) So, I just wanted to say, 'Thank you, Marc,' and that is all I have to say."

The funeral was a silent nightmare. The thought of putting Marie's body in the ground was almost more than I could bear. Robert sat by me all the time and that was some help but not much. I never heard a word the preacher said.

After the funeral, I drove home with Robert. Not a word was said, until he said, "You mean I got to forgive Arthur?" I said, quietly. " No, you don't have to forgive. It just depends on whether you want to be happy or not."

When we pulled up in the driveway , Robert said, "I think I will go and practice the organ for a while." I did not go and listen, but I could only imagine how beautiful the concert would be.

Bluebonnets

It is that time again. Hit me like a spring shower. I said to myself. "What have I been doing? What in the world? "I had not expected, or even paid attention to, the seasons coming and going. Head down, in a hurry, back and forth to the office almost unconscious while making the same journey every single, solitary day. I walked with my head down and refused to acknowledge that the summer was over, and the leaves were changing, and (hard to believe) the weather was getting cooler.

Still immersed in my thoughts and without even looking up, I suddenly came to a small patch of bright blue flowers on the edge of the walk, blooming completely out of season. The color was so brilliant, it almost shouted. I had to stop. The voice of the extreme color had almost hit my heart. Suddenly, from out of nowhere, a voice pierced my silence like a knife, when I heard the words, "Shocking, isn't it? I was just going to pick one when I saw you stop. I could not pass without touching them."

With that, she bent over and picked one single flower, handed it to me, and said, "And that my friend is a lupinus texensis," as she turned and walked away. " It is Texas' favorite flower, although few people know its name." And before I knew it, she was gone.

I had to run to catch her because she walked away so fast. She moved at such a rapid pace and was already at the intersection and starting across the street. I began to chase her and laughed when I was by her side. I almost had to shout because the traffic noise was so loud, "I wasn't really flirting with you—just thought it was funny that you could see the flowers and even more that you would stop to look."

"I would rather have heard that you were flirting." She laughed and said, without even looking at me.. She laughed again, "Oh, I know how to do that, and sometimes I let myself. It makes my fiancé mad, but he gets over it. Who in the world are you, and why are you flirting with me?"

"Because it's Thursday and that is my day to flirt—the only day, I might add. It infuriates Elizabeth, my fiancé. Do you have time for a cup of coffee?" As I gestured to the coffee bar on the corner. "Don't want this flirting to go too far. —Will you take the time, or are you too busy? — You have to pay for the coffee."

She slapped me on the shoulder and said, "Cheapskate! You pay or I will never speak to you again." We stopped and stood facing each other in the middle of the street. The traffic stopped, and a few blew their horns.

I grabbed her hand, started to the curb, and said, "How about coffee here next Thursday, same time, same place?"

She nodded her head, leaned back, laughed, and said, "It's a deal." As she turned to rush across the street, I shouted, "My name is Robert. What's yours?"

She looked over her shoulder and smiled, "I'm Michelle. Michelle Stevens."

I could hardly believe what had happened, and realized I had made an appointment with a woman I did not know—-Was that crazy, or what?"

That week, dragged by so slowly I could barely count the days but before I knew it, it was Thursday, I laughed to myself, Was I going? "Of course not. She would not be there."

I began to sort out the mail on my desk and before I even realized what I was doing, I had my coat and was out the door. I practically ran to the coffee bar, went inside, looked up and down every aisle — I walked through the crowd, looking everywhere for her, but she was nowhere to be found. I thought, "Oh well, you should have known she would not come—chance meeting on the street. Crazy to even expect her to meet a total stranger."

I started to leave, and as I was going out the door, I nearly ran into her as she was entering the coffee bar. She said, "Oh, you were leaving?"

I said, "Of course not, I was just looking for you. Are you always late to your appointments?"

"Just on this one day," as she glanced at me out of the corner of her eyes.

We found our seats and were drinking coffee and I said, "How in the world did you come to know the botanical name for a blue bonnet?"

"That is a long story, but here is the short version. My father died suddenly, unexpectedly and my mother, to deal with her grief, started studying flowering plants. She built a huge greenhouse in our back yard. You ought to see it—-blows your mind. But she has dealt—is dealing—with her grief."

"Never heard of that but it sounds like a great idea." While she explained, for the first time I stopped and really looked at this woman and she was beautiful. I was amazed and could not believe I had not paid attention to her beauty. What in the world was the matter with me? It was usually the first thing I looked for. I was stunned and reached out and held her hand. I asked, "Michelle, what would it take for me to interfere with the relationship you are in right now?"

She said, "Well, I don't know, but you said you were in a relationship also. What can you do about that?"

"That would only take a couple of years. How long can you wait?" And I smiled and took her hand.

"You don't work very fast, do you? I think I could be ready in a year." She stood very slowly, as if she were leaving.

I said, "Wait just a minute. What about this weekend? I will pick you up Friday night at 7:30, that is, if you will give me an address."

Then I said, "Michelle, my relationship has been dead for a long time, and I am ready to end it now. She is probably as bored as I am, but neither of us will admit this. We stopped being honest long ago, I think

I even know the time." Couldn't believe I was saying this. Guess I had not been honest with myself for some time."

She laughed heartily and said. "Join the club, Robert. I was going to say exactly the same thing." All of sudden, she was deadly serious, and said, "Do you think you could be honest with me?" She sat back down, and I was relieved.

I turned my head and took a sip of coffee. "Lady, before I answer, do you believe in miracles?"

Her answer puzzled me when she said, "Not unless I can deny what is happening right now. I am shocked at what I have been thinking since I met you." She hit me on the shoulder and said, "You have ruined my sleep. Get out of my bedroom."

I repeated, "Do you believe in miracles? Do you believe it was an accident that someone planted that flower in that exact spot so that you would see it and even know the real name? Just so that you and I would meet at that exact spot at the exact moment. Did it surprise you that we both drink coffee?" I poured out the questions.

She stood, walked around the table, and sat in my lap. Everyone near us cheered and applauded. She jumped up very quickly and then, to my amazement, took a bow and curtsied to the crowd. The applause was twice as large at this time. She sat down, blushed and hid her face in her hands. I was dumbfounded and did not know what to say or do.

I surprised myself when I stood, raised my cup, and said, "Coffee for everyone in the house. My treat." The applause and cheering was deafening. We finished our coffee and when we stood to walk out there was still some limited applause.

Once outside, I said, "Well, that was a cup of coffee. I don't know what we can do for an encore." She grabbed my hand and started walking. I asked, "Where are we going?

She said, "I don't know. Doesn't matter. Do you have a car?"

I said, "No. Riding the bus today."

With that, we stopped at the next bus stop and boarded the bus. "End of the line." She told the driver and gave him a bill.

We found seats and she snuggled close to me.

I leaned over and she whispered, "What is your last name?"

I said, "It will be Blackwell after we marry."

She was not shocked but simply said, "Please spell that. I might need to know," and then as she held out her left hand, she said, "Where's my ring?"

"Next bus stop. Let's get off." and we both exited the bus, walked across the street and into a jewelry store. Just inside the store, she stopped. held both my hands and faced me. "We must stop. Are you crazy? Are you thinking marriage? What in the world? Are you serious?"

"Never been more serious in my life. Although I am not sure, right now, that I am sane. I have never in my life met anyone like you just in the minutes...seconds I have known you. I have been looking for you forever. Where in the world have you been? Can't believe I finally found you. Be still. Don't move. Don't vanish."

The jeweler cleared his throat, to get our attention. We walked over, and I said, "We would like to look at wedding rings."

He put several pairs on the counter, and we tried them and looked at each other. Tears were streaming down her face. The man behind the counter disappeared. We stood, just for a moment and I asked, "Will you marry me and be my wife until death doth us part?" I got down on my knees and said, "I promise to be the best husband I am capable of being."

To my surprise, she got down on her knees and made a similar promise. We both stayed there for just a moment. I stood and helped her to stand, and we hugged and kissed there in the jewelry store for the very first time. Strange, we both forgot we were in a public place, as we stood there both crying. The man behind the counter disappeared again and we laughed and called him back. We chose the same rings, as both of us liked the same ones.

The man behind the counter, cleared his throat, coughed twice, and said, "The rings can be returned in thirty days.— Just want you to know."

I said, "Not in 30 years." and we hurried out of the store.

"I have a feeling that maybe we need to talk with your mother." I suddenly blurted out, although I was a little anxious at the thought.

Michelle said, "Good, let's go." as we boarded the bus for her home.

We were getting off in just a moment and walking up to her front door. Michelle called her mother and said immediately, "Mother, Robert and I have fallen in love, bought rings, and are going to get married."

Her mother took a step back and said, "Well, that is quite a handful, do you think we could sit down?"

I said, "Mrs. Stevens, I know this is a shock to you. It was to us. But we wanted you to know and talk to you before the wedding and make whatever plans you felt necessary, We did not, by any means, plan to leave you out. We will respect your needs and wishes in everything we do and plan.

"But how long have you known each other? What kind of work do you do? Have you been married before?" She was filled with questions as she poured them all right out. Michelle laughed and put her arms around her mother.

Then I heard her say," Mother I have been looking for this man for twenty-nine years and finally found him just a few days ago. I knew him instantly—I could not miss him after looking for twenty-nine years."

"But what about Raymond?" Her mother was puzzled.

"Haven't ever loved him like I do this man right here." And Michelle hugged me as she spoke.

Her mother smiled and said, "Well, my dear, I have never said this, but I always thought Raymond was a dud. Just didn't want to say it because you were dating him."

"Mother, would you show Robert your greenhouse please?" Michelle was trying to make an impression, and I knew it. We immediately went outside, and the entire backyard was under one single roof. We walked in and looked all around. It was quite a sight and I enjoyed seeing it. I could tell that Michelle was proud also. We walked around, looked at hundreds of plants, until her mother grew tired and suggested we have tea.

Back inside the house we sat and talked briefly. Her mother asked, "Robert, what kind of work do you do?"

I answered, "I am an attorney and have been for a few years since I finished law school. I have my own firm with two other guys. We have worked together for several years and believe it or not, we like each other and work well together. I consider both of them as friends."

After we had tea, Michelle suggested we go for a walk. I felt a strong need to tell her that I was a Christian, but for some reason I was a little hesitant. As we walked, I said, "I need to tell you something very important to me. Are you ready?"

She was very quiet and said, "This has an ominous sound. Tell me quickly."

I held her hand and said, "I am a Christian, and have been since I was a sophomore in college. An atheist when I started college but after I arrived, I met other students who were happy and healthy individuals. I finally, not quickly. came to believe in Jesus Christ. Since then, I have tried to live the way I thought a Christian should. I go to church regularly and meet with several Christian groups during the week. You need to know this is deep in my heart and precious in my life."

Michelle was quiet for a long time. Finally, she took my hand and said, "I have not had the experiences you have had but I am certainly willing to learn. Are you willing to be patient with me and give me time to learn?"

I had to catch my breath and then I said, "My heart fairly sang when you said those words. Of course, my dear, I am in no hurry, and we are not going anywhere separately. We will travel together everywhere we go. I have been alone long enough, I assure you. I am fed up with the term 'single,' I am ready to share my life with you, my dear, and more than ready. Now that I have found you. I thank God for bringing us together."

I was so happy with her response. I had been afraid she would be threatened by the question. Then I heard, "Robert, I am a learner and willing to hear and accept new information. We both must learn about the other person. Please don't be afraid to tell me anything about yourself. I will do the same."

I laughed and said, "Well, you might as well know, I am a hoarder or have been for the last few years, and I have been hoarding dollars so I could buy a home. Did not know when or what I wanted, and I am glad I have you to show me what to do with this money."

She laughed loudly, "I would love to look at houses with you. Let's go right now."

I said, "Wait just a minute. I have a good friend who is a realtor. Can we talk with her first? Do you mind?"

"Not at all, Give her a call right now" was my immediate response.

Marie, the realtor, was there in minutes. She hugged me, which surprised Michelle.

As we drove away, she said, "You hit me at just the right time. I have three wonderful properties that you will absolutely love. But you can't be greedy. I will only sell you one. You can't have all three. Have you set a date yet?" Then she looked at me and said, "Girl you are getting a wonderful man. I wanted to marry him myself until I found someone nicer and married him. You will get to meet him, I am sure."

We pulled into a driveway and saw a beautiful house. Marie was right. It was a real looker. We went inside but I was not impressed. The next house was really a dream, to Michelle. I was quiet for a while and thought I would wait to see what Michelle said. She walked all around the house, went in every room. Then she came back to me and said, "What do you think?"

I was almost bursting with desire and said, "You go first."

And she said, "It's a go for me, I really like it. Even the price is right."

We did not go to look at the third house. We were both pleased with this one we had just found.

We got the keys to go back and get Michelle's mother to look with us. She fell in love with the house instantly. She insisted that she would make the down payment. We both thanked her for the offer. I was personally glad to get her approval but surprised to get even more.

Michelle and I took a short drive and talked about the future. Then she said. 'Do you think maybe, perhaps... we should talk about a wedding?"

We both laughed, and I said, "Great idea. Let's do that."

I pulled into a drive-in restaurant so we could eat. We looked at each other for a long time and then burst out laughing. I said, "Well. at least we waited to have a child. Lots of couples don't even do that."

Michelle grew silent and teared up just a little. She dropped her head and said, "I had my tubes tied a few years ago. I am sure that can be undone, but I don't know."

I said, "Well, we can find out easily by asking your doctor."

Michelle remained quiet for a few minutes and said, "Robert, I did not mean to deceive you, but we do need to get this information because if I can't have a child, you need to know."

I walked around the table stood her up and said, "I am marrying you, as you are, where you are, who you are, any way you are, and childbearing or not is not an option." I kissed her on the lips, popped her on her rear, and took my seat just before she ran around the table and fell in my lap. She threw her arms around me and hugged me for the longest time.

I was happier than I could ever remember in my entire life.

We decided on a small wedding in the church. I talked to my minister, and he said he would be glad to officiate. I told him that I was nervous and anxious about being married, and he suggested that I call Michelle and talk through those feelings.

I took his advice and immediately called Michelle. She said, "Come right over here, right now." In no time I was at her door which she opened, gave me a hug and a kiss and we walked out on the patio where she had a pot of coffee and two cups waiting just for us.

I told her about my nervousness and my fear. She listened for a few moments and then began to laugh. She laughed just a moment and then she began to cry as she told me she had the same feelings—-did not know how to be married, had never had sex with anyone and did not know how to cook. We both began to laugh, to the point of hysteria.

Her fears were almost identical to mine.

By the time we finished talking both of us were relieved and laughing. It was a wonderful visit and we both dealt with our anxiety and our fears. Then Michelle said, "Maybe this is what marriage is all about—-you have someone to talk with and do not have to solve your problems alone." I was so relieved; I was weak and sat down by her side while we both laughed, hugged, and kissed. Her mother came out, then quickly apologized and went back in the house.

Our wedding was a dream. There was no one there but us and two witnesses. The minister's words were perfect and specifically appropriate for the two of us. The ceremony was very meaningful, and Michelle's tears seems to add to the beauty of the moment. I was surprised to see myself crying during the ceremony. It was a sacred moment for both of us.

Time passed very quickly. The wedding was over. And soon we were on a flight to Hawaii for a two-week honeymoon, with hopefully some rest while we were there. We were so excited and felt that everyone could tell that we had just married and were on our honeymoon.

The plane had barely left the airport when we heard an announcement from the captain, "Ladies and Gentlemen, please do not be alarmed, but we must return to the terminal. There is no danger just a routine problem and we will be touching down in just a few minutes."

The plane landed easily, and we were asked to take our bags with us. All the passengers unloaded. Everyone seemed at ease about the return to the terminal. We decided to eat dinner while we were waiting for news about the next flight. I was surprised by the way Michelle handled the interruption. After dinner, she went in the newsstand and began to look at magazines. I was surprised and excited with this woman. She was another world, and I was amused and challenged with her.

Hours later, after we reboarded the flight, the captain apologized for the delay, and we were finally on our way. In seconds, we both were sound asleep. The announcement that we were landing awakened both of us. We finally landed in Hawaii and quickly found the limo to our hotel. We checked in very quickly and went to our suite.

We sat on the beach for hours and hours. We did not need or want to go back to our room. The very word "honeymoon" kept ringing in my mind and was a dream and to be on the beach in Hawaii. We ran into an older couple who said, "We are here for our 50th wedding anniversary." They had children older than we were and when we walked away and looked back, they were kissing.

We watched the sun slip quietly into the ocean then went inside the hotel for our evening meal. We immediately ran into the older couple (Mr. and Mrs. Mickelson from Augusta, Georgia) and they insisted we eat with them. We did, and we had a hilarious evening. I found myself wishing I would have that kind of attitude at their age.

Sometime later,— two, maybe three, four days later,— we emerged from our suite to go sight- seeing, and I heard Michelle calling herself, my "wife." We laughed every minute from sheer joy. ...No reason, just the wonder and the joy and the thrill of being together. I never dreamed that this would be what marriage was. (The marriages I had dealt with in the office were not like ours.)

I said to myself "Hey man, this is still the honeymoon, don't lose your bearings," but the magic did not disappear. She was spontaneous, focused, loving, attentive, and, and, and...playful to a point that absolutely astounded me. We took a helicopter flight and saw beautiful views of the island and the city. I was never bored one single moment—-At times I was challenged or shocked or...something... but never bored.

Upon our return home, I learned that our firm had been asked to assist in an international trial. There would be a lot of publicity, which meant status for our firm. Everyone on the staff had to begin a study of International Law, specifically law procedures of France. I was gone from Michelle many hours during the day.

As things proceeded, we moved to Paris very quickly. I was at the office constantly. Michelle was a good sport and found ways to fill her time. In fact, on some days she came and studied with me at the French National Library. The French courtroom was very, very different from ours. For practice, Michelle and I went through some trial procedures when we were at home. On some days we practiced with the other attorneys who were on our staff and studying, just like I was.

I had not studied French in high school or college like some of the other members on the firm had done. Michelle would not allow me to get discouraged but insisted that I stay on top of this deal all the time. We wanted to do whatever was necessary to help our client win the case in France; however, I had some serious reservations. The more we studied and prepared the more we realized it was necessary to employ a French firm to help with the work. We soon had contact with a firm that came highly recommended and were ready to move forward.

It became necessary, however, for a member of our firm to be in Paris for the trial. Michelle was ready and eager to stay, so we stayed to represent our firm. I was to be the *avocat* from America in the proce en salle d'audience.

We found an apartment which we rented for six months. Michelle was thrilled at the thought of having time in Paris without responsibility. We shopped for several days, visited several restaurants, and saw shows in the evenings. It was a wonderful vacation for both of us.

The trial date was postponed several times, which we expected, and this gave us more play- time to see the city. Several times, I visited the French law firm that would be representing us. There was not a lot for me to do because of my limited knowledge of the language. I did simplify matters to some degree when I purchased an instant translator (about the size of my cell phone). This was a significant help for both Michelle and for me.

Time finally arrived for the trial to begin. To our surprise a jury was sworn in, and the interrogation of witnesses began. Michelle shopped or stayed in the apartment watching the TV most of the day. I stopped by the "greengrocer" on the way home each day. The trial progressed very slowly, and it seemed we would be in Paris much longer than we had expected. We talked about the possibility of Michelle going home, but she vetoed the idea and chose to stay with me. I was elated. She said she would stay forever rather than leave me. I was unbelievably proud and happy.

The trial got very complicated and involved. Many witnesses were called in, which I had not expected. The language, of course, was a problem since I could not understand even half of what was being said. But I sat, listened, listened, and listened. One member of the French firm was very kind and came periodically to give me updates about what was going on. She was a beautiful lady named Monica that was very kind to both Michelle and to me. Several evenings she visited with Michelle, which was a great help.

The judge called a two-weeks recess in the trial. We decided to visit Switzerland and go skiing. Great fun, but it was very different from skiing in America. I quickly discovered that Michelle was a much better skier than I, but I managed to hold my own, I did hire a teacher to stay with me on the big runs. But I managed to keep up even though it was difficult.

We were both sorry when the two weeks ended. The train, of course, was filled with skiers and the trip back to Paris was all fun and games. We were surrounded when the crowd found we were from the States. The trip back and forth was very nice and we enjoyed it both ways.

Back in court, I sat through a long and boring day with witnesses being called and interrogated. Finally, the day was over, I stopped by the greengrocer to pick up a few things and headed home. I rang the doorbell before I unlocked the door like I usually did. As I opened the door and walked in, I called for Michelle. There was no answer and the silence fairly screamed at me. I ran from room to room frantically searching for my wife, but the apartment was completely empty. I stood still, totally shocked, unable to think, move, or talk. A sense of panic swept over me, and I stood completely immobile in the middle of the apartment. I thought immediately of Monica, found my phone, and called her but there was no answer. I called the office and understood that there was an emergency number that I could call. I tried that number but could not understand the message.

There was no one to call. I did not understand the language and there was nowhere I could call. I felt completely, absolutely, totally lost and alone. I stood in the middle of the room and, something like "Gustavipos" kept running through my mind. I found a phone book and began to look through the long list of *avocats*. There were several listings under the same name and so I started calling from the top. There was no answer when I called any of the numbers, so I started again calling the very first number. Someone answered and hung up quickly when they could not understand what I was saying. I called back as soon as the person hung up and said "Merci, merci, merci," over and over until the person held the line open and tried to talk with me. I think the person said for me to wait.

In just a minute someone started talking in perfect English and I heard, "Can I help you?" I began to explain as best I could what the situation was and then I was transferred to another person who began to take down my information.

I wanted to scream, "Somebody do something. I need help. Not talk. Please, for Pete's sake, somebody help me!!!"

After about an hour, my doorbell rang, and I went to the door and saw a person dressed in civilian clothes. He showed me his credentials proving he was a police officer. I asked him inside and the questioning began: "How long have you been married? How old is your wife? Did you have an argument this morning before you left? Do you have a picture?"

I had no response because I know Michelle would not have left the house without letting me know. The phone rang. It was Mr. Gustavipos, the head of the firm that had taken our case to trial. He asked if he could come over and of course, I invited him. In a matter of minutes, he was at the door with several friends, one of whom was the Police Commissioner for the city of Paris. The other two were detectives. I gave them all the information they asked for, but I did not feel any better about Michelle. I kept saying to myself, "This cannot be true, it just cannot be happening to us. It is not...it cannot be true... I will wake up in a moment and it will all be over...." But it did not happen that way. It was true and it was happening to me.

The hours and minutes had leaden feet and dragged across the face of time like they had no intention of moving. We sat in the room. Mr. Gustavipos got an occasional call but did not explain its purpose. Finally, he looked at the Commissioner of police and said, "The people we are in trial with are from Tuscovia. I know nothing about them but have heard that they are vicious. I have heard several bad reports from that direction. I have no idea if they are involved in this, but it needs to be checked out." I was very impatient and not interested in talk—I wanted to find Michelle. The thought of her being in the hands of dangerous foreigners almost drove me crazy. Two or three days passed and there was no sign or news from Michelle. I stayed at police headquarters waiting for some word, but none ever came.

In desperation, I hired two private investigation firms and after three days, got no results. I did not tell anyone because I knew of the jealously that existed between these people and the police. One more wasted effort to find my Michelle. I thought I would lose my mind if I could not find her.

Finally, a call came from the police saying, "We have located a body that fits the description of your wife. Can you come and identify? I was desperate every minute until I got to the police morgue.

I went in and a uniformed police officer met me and said, "This woman is not dead. It appeared that she was dead when she was first discovered, but we began to see signs of life after she was moved. There is very little indication that she will survive. Please talk to the police surgeon with you when you go to see the body."

The trip to the morgue took a thousand years but finally we were there. I could hardly walk but I did, only with the aid of two police officers who walked with me. When we reached the slab that held the body, a doctor was standing nearby with a stethoscope. He stopped and shook hands with me. I didn't want to touch him. I had to refrain to keep from choking him.

The minute I saw Michelle, I knew immediately it was her and I leaned over and kissed her cold lips. The doctor stepped up and said, "Both arms and both legs are broken. She is presently in a state of shock."

I said, "For God's sake let's get her to the hospital." Two attendants came in with a stretcher mounted on wheels and were moving the "body." I walked beside her so I could hold her hand. My heart, soul, mind, and body were screaming, "Please God, do not let this woman die." Please...please...please...please" was all that I could say or think. There was no movement, and her hand was ice cold.

I insisted that they get blankets to cover and warm her body and was told it was best for "the body" to stay cold. I wanted to scream and say that is not just a "body"...it is MY wife, but I chose to remain quiet. I asked the doctor why it was necessary for her to stay cold, and he said," We must maintain the state of shock until her heart gets back to normal."

I stood there and held her hand; that seemed to be all that I could do now, and I kept saying; "God, please...God, please...God, please"...over and over and over." My body turned cold, just like hers, and I did not want to be warm.

Time passed...I do not know how long...I stood ...and stood...forever...until...finally, after days, days, days, centuries, and eons......the doctor came and examined "the body" and then began putting blankets on her. It was such a relief, and my own body began to get warmer. I kept watching her face for any sign of life and saw nothing that looked like a positive sign. I kept praying and praying without stopping... "Please God"...over and over.

Finally...finally...like forever, I could feel just a little warmth in her hand. I brushed back her hair, careful not to touch her face and whispered, "This is Robert. You are safe. I love you. I am here beside you." There was no response. I waited and waited and waited—-no response of any kind. I asked the doctor "Why?"

He said, "She is not capable—maybe in two or three hours. Don't rush it. Your wife is better. I can tell you. She will live. At least, for the present. I can say that." I stepped away so that I would not interfere. I prayed and prayed and prayed. I had taken a seat next to the wall and the doctor walked over to me and said, "Would you go home and rest if I promise you, I will stay right here, by her side, until you return?"

I looked at him for a moment and told him I would leave. I gave him my phone number and left. The trip back to our apartment took hours and hours, or it seemed that way to me, but when I walked in the bedroom, I fell on the bed, went to sleep, and slept forever.

I have no idea how long I slept. It seemed like forever, so I was totally disoriented when I was awakened by the ringing of my phone. It was the doctor (He said his name was O'Brian). He said Michelle was showing signs of waking up and he thought I should be there.

I left immediately and was off to the hospital where she had been transferred. I rushed to the room and looked for the number on the door where she had been assigned. Dr. O'Brian was standing outside. He put his hand on my shoulder and said, "Be absolutely calm, not one ounce of excitement—-absolutely no excitement of any kind whatever she says or whatever you feel. If she begins to get upset, hold her hand, reassure her that you are there and as soon as you can, leave the room. You will not be able to calm her. We will do that with medication.

I went in and stood by the bed. I did not say a word. Slowly, very slowly, she tried to turn her head to look at me. I leaned over and kissed her very gently. I saw no response. I wanted to pick her up and hold her but did not dare. I reached for her hand but was immediately stopped by a nurse standing close by. She whispered to me, "Both arms are broken. Both legs are broken." Dr. O'Brian stepped forward and moved the nurse back.

He put his finger to his lips, and I knew he was telling me to be quiet. I stepped back from the bed and let the doctor and the nurse get closer. It took several minutes for them to take care of Michelle, and I was ushered outside. Waiting outside was hard, but I knew it was necessary and waited and waited. I heard her scream several times and it was hard to restrain myself and not go in the room. However, I waited and stayed outside.

The doctor came out and said they were going to take her to surgery for a while and I needed to leave and come back later. It was hard to leave but I made the decision to walk down the Champs-Elysees because there are lots of sights on that street. I walked and walked and walked but my mind was always back in the hospital with Michelle in surgery. After a long walk I re-entered the hospital and found out she was in recovery. More waiting and waiting and waiting, about an hour later a nurse came out and said, in terrible English, that she was asleep.

I was almost desperate to see her and finally was admitted to her room. She was in a cast up to her waist and both arms were in casts. The doctor stood by me and explained what had been done. I was speechless after he had finished and could not understand how she had survived the torture. It had been torture, which I had not been told about, at the request of the police. I could not believe they had cut her and burned her arms and legs. I hoped that the drugs would dull the pain. There was no more denying. Here she is now in front of me and in terrible shape. I worked hard to keep from screaming at the top of my lungs. That was part of me, and another part wanted to get a gun, find them, and shoot them into little pieces.

The visiting hours were over, and I had to leave. I went straight to police headquarters to make inquiry about this incident. I talked with three officers, two from The *Gendarmerie Nationale,* on the case and they were willing to talk to me. The language, of course, was limited, but as far as I could understand, the people in Tuscovia had an intense hatred for the French and resented being under their control. It was clear that we had become involved with an international situation that had nothing to do with us, I had no idea how they found Michelle except the newspapers had been filled with every detail of our arrival.

They found out that Michelle was a very important person, or rather thought she was. They assumed she was French. They planned the kidnapping. They had also planned a huge revolution (that did not materialize) the next day. They were very primitive people and still engaged in many small tribal wars and took pride in torturing their enemies.

I was constantly at the hospital with concerns for the healing of her legs and arms. She started physical therapy before she was out of the casts. I protested and was told politely to please step outside and wait until the treatment was over.

The chaplain made regular visits and she looked forward to the time with him and seemed to enjoy talking with him. I sat in on several visits and enjoyed listening to their conversation. Michelle had a constant stream of questions, and I was amazed at her understanding. She was possessed about learning more and more about Jesus of Nazareth. She read and reread everything given to her that told her about his life and teaching.

Months later, that seemed like years, I was told that they would remove the casts. Had no idea how painful that would be, and I had to leave the room when it was being done. The doctors and nurses were very kind and exceedingly patient. I was impressed with the way Michelle tolerated the pain. I was told that they would do skin grafts to cover the burns.

The doctor himself, at one point, walked over to me, and said, "You, my friend, are married to an unusual lady." She will emerge from this entire experience with a minimal amount of damage. She has a spirit that I have seen only rarely in this, or any hospital."

I was very proud and asked if he had told Michelle and he said, "Yes, many times."

Physical therapy every day, every day, every day,.. it seemed like forever. The technicians were very patient with her, and I stood very close while she was being helped.

She made remarkable progress, except on the first day she tried to walk, which was very, very difficult and very painful. She did manage to stand for a second. and we all cheered very loudly. There seemed to be more pain in her arms and arm movement. It was a bigger challenge than walking.

While we were still in the rehab hospital the French Ambassador called and made an appointment to visit with Michelle and requested that her family be present. Four men came with the ambassador, and they made inquiries about Michelle's condition.

Everyone was seated and the ambassador apologized for the event and said they had collected damages from the country of Tuscovia and that they had been paid in gold. He then said, "I have brought you a check for four million, seven hundred seventy-eight thousand, three hundred and seventy-five francs and I hope you will be kind enough to accept this with our apology for this very unfortunate accident. Of course, we do not expect money to fully compensate us for the damage. We do want, again, to extend our sincere apology for this unfortunate incident. This does not properly represent the way we treat visitors to our country and again we apologize for the action of the crazies in Tuscovia."

With that, the entire delegation left, and Michelle turned to me and said, "I know exactly what I am going to do with the money. I can hardly wait to get started."

I volunteered, "I hope you will learn to function with arms and legs before you decide to change the world."

"I plan to do just exactly that," Michelle said laughing loudly as we walked into the room where her hospital bed had been located. I heard her singing softly as she checked her bandages. This was a huge step forward for Michelle, and I could not imagine her singing.

Several days later she was free to go back to our apartment. Her mother wanted her to go home to the States. of course. She even made several calls from the vehicle which took us home. this woman amazed me. I was very puzzled hearing only one side of a conversation but pleased when Michelle talked about construction and purchase of property even though I had no idea what she was thinking and planning. I insisted that she tell me something of her plans although I could not press very hard on anything. She cried very easily, and I tried to be careful and patient. Her doctor had told me to expect this. It was still difficult to see her in this condition.

Michele's mother had come over from the States very soon after we found her. She was very stable and mature and was a big help for me. Being in her presence was a tremendous help for me because I found it still difficult to control my emotions. When I thought about the amount of money, it was shocking to me, and I could not imagine what the two of us would do with that much money.

On Saturday, the end of the week Michelle suddenly announced that she wanted to talk with everyone on Monday. She even asked that a representative from the French embassy be present. I could not, in my wildest imagination, decide what she had in mind. I asked her mother if she knew and she said, "No idea." We waited and wondered what she would say.

Monday came and everyone was seated in the parlor waiting for Michelle's speech. She was rolled in with the wheelchair and stayed in the center of the room. She closed her eyes and bowed her head. Then she asked me to come and stand by her for just a moment. I quickly moved over and held her hand.

She began very slowly as she said, "I ask in advance for your understanding and your tolerance because I do not understand myself what I am going to say. So, I certainly will not expect you to understand what I do not understand myself. But here goes: I have felt several times in the past weeks that I was dying, or already dead. You will understand if I do not try to explain. I do not know, but it seems that I did a sort of evaluation of my life. I am looking for an effective way to say this, but God was there in my mind. I cannot tell you a form or shape—just take what I said. My life, for a while, was over; it had ended. I stood for a moment and heard the question, 'What did you do with your life?' I had no answer for the question. I remember no feelings except remorse, at that point. Somewhere in this maze of confusion, I could see the black bodies of my persecutors. To my surprise, I did not hate them, even when I was aware of the pain. I think...I think...though I am...not sure of this at all...I think I felt compassion for the people who were injuring my body. This did not diminish the pain.

It may be one of the times I felt I had died." (Michelle's mother began to crumble at this point and someone helped her to a chair.)

Michelle continued, "All this time, I kept hearing words I did not understand, 'If a person smite thee on one cheek, turn to him the other also.' For some reason that I do not understand, I knew exactly what the words meant for me. It seems ,though I am not so sure of this, that the cuts on my body did not hurt anymore.

"Having said this, I want to say that I plan to go to Tuscovia. I will use some of the money allocated to me to build orphanages and a hospital, depending on my finances. I plan to repay the pain and injury with kindness. I will, as best I can, 'turn the other cheek,' though I am not sure I understand what I am saying. I talked with the chaplain at length about this plan. I hope to be able to communicate this to the people of Tuscovia in a manner that they will understand. I know that will be difficult, but I will make the effort."

Michelle paused for a moment, wiped the tears from her eyes and continued. "In conclusion, I want to say that instead of getting revenge for what happened to me ——I will kiss them on the cheek. If I understand anything at all about this man, Jesus, this is what He would have done. I think this is the way He dealt with the crucifixion. (I remember and I re-read that He said, 'Father, forgive them, for they know not what they do.' I hope you will understand what I am trying to do, even though I am sure it is hard for you to understand. I am not completely sure I know myself." The room was deathly quiet. No one moved or said a word. A nurse helped Michelle position herself in the wheelchair to make her more comfortable.

The representative from the French embassy said, " My country will add two hundred fifty thousand francs toward this effort." Several other people began to write checks and give them to Michelle. The air in the room was electric as everyone stood and waited for Michelle to be taken out of the room. The silence was deafening.

Michelle's mother stood and said, "I will contribute one hundred thousand francs to this effort." Of course, the newspapers quickly found out about Michelle's speech and began to spread the news. The general public was amazed, particularly the people of Tuscovia were totally stunned when they heard her remarks. Some of the people were calling for her to be president of the country, which of course was impossible. When news reports were read to Michelle, she only smiled. I wondered many times what was actually going on in her mind.

Michelle had arranged to meet with several architects to look at plans for the orphanage buildings. They met in a reception area so they could use video setups. I stayed with her the entire afternoon, and she did not seem to tire one bit during the process. It was finally decided to have three dormitories and one school building in the middle of a quadrangle. Talking to Ralph, who had recently joined our group as the accountant, we found we were still close to the budget. However, it soon became clear that we would need more money as the plans developed.

To my complete surprise , Michelle said she was going to meet with the People's Congress, a governing body in Tuscovia, elected annually by popular vote. I could not believe she planned to address the group in person. Over our protests she made plans and got permission to speak at the next meeting. The nurses and the medical staff arranged for her comfort during the trip and also during the session. Her determination and courage was an inspiration to the entire group. She never showed signs of fatigue. Dr. Snowden angrily insisted that she go away and rest at one point. The final evening session was a crucial point for the entire program. She stood and spoke with perfect poise and clarity. The local citizenry were hypnotized by her presence.

At the end of the meeting, she called for a vote and unexpectedly got unanimous approval for the entire program exactly as submitted. It was at this point that a splinter group began to develop and provided opposition to every single recommendation. It became obvious that the meeting would end in confusion. The splinter group began to yell and shout and would not allow anyone to address the meeting.

Michelle dismissed everyone except the splinter group which left about twenty people in the room. Then she stood and said, "You are primitive people because you are uneducated and if you continue this way, then you will be like this forever. Now sit down and shut up and allow some progress to be made in this meeting. If you do not do this, I am leaving and will not do anything to help the country. Now get out of the building and do not return until you are ready to keep your mouths shut."

The interpreter, a native, laughed uncontrollably when she had finished, and all the people filed slowly out of the building. When the group returned there was total silence. Michelle stood and went over the entire program without a single question. The loudest voice in the splinter group from now on was a very large lady (named Ella) who stood immediately and told Michelle she would be her "leader for the rest of the time" and the crowd applauded.

I watched in amazement as Michelle handled every situation that arose. But I became increasingly aware that Michelle had withdrawn from me. I tried to talk with her about this at night when the two of us were alone and she said she was tired and did not feel like talking. I began to withdraw, inappropriately; I knew I should not. I went and talked to Dr. Andrews, her doctor. He said, "I had expected this because in lots of instances where an injury was traumatic, like Michelle's, I have seen a total change in personality. Now I have a recommendation which you will not like and may prefer not to do but it is my recommendation."

I said, "Please let me hear it."

The doctor said, "Go away for two weeks. I will stay in contact with Michelle and make some lame excuse about why you are away. I will tell you when to return. I do not promise my plan will work, sometimes it does and sometimes it does not."

Reluctantly, I went to Switzerland to ski in the Alps. It was hard because I was worried about Michelle, but I had to admit, I was having fun. I had a lot of fun socializing in the evenings in the pub filled with ski bums. After two weeks, I got a call from the doctor, and he suggested I stay another week. I had no choice but to take his suggestion and stay.

Dr. Andrews said "I have not seen any progress. Tell me about the first time you met Michelle. Something that would remind her of the good times in the past. I hope I can help but the trauma Michelle has experienced sometimes changes personality.

I told him about the bluebonnets, and he roared with laughter. Then he said, "Find a florist and send her an armload."

I called everywhere until I found a florist that could deliver an armload of bluebonnets. They were to be delivered two days later.

I got a call. Michelle was exuberant. She had just received the flowers and was in total shock. It was the old Michelle, just like before. I could hardly contain myself and I said, "Lupinus texenesis" and heard her scream. I was overjoyed and made plans to go back home on the next train. I also called the doctor and told him the results.

When the train arrived, I went straight to the rehab hospital. She said she was ready to go home as soon as I walked in the door. We talked to the doctors and decided to wait one more week, but she responded to me in a way she had not responded since the accident.

We talked to the doctors and nurses, and they agreed it was time for Michelle to leave the hospital whenever she desired, but she would need a nurse for a while. So off we went.

In the ambulance and on the way home, we celebrated every mile. I was overjoyed and the nurse was a dream help. Michelle was in good spirits, and I felt we could start living again. Having the nurse was a huge help, and Michelle felt a lot more comfortable with her there.

The next day, Michelle wanted to go and look at the first stages of construction. We drove for a long time. We did not see much but Michelle was very excited when we arrived at the spot where the dormitories were going to be constructed.

Several weeks later, lots of progress had been made. We had a town-hall meeting to decide how the new project would be run. The meeting went well without interruption. There were lots of applications for employment as matrons in the dormitories and janitors. It was decided that we would send the first employees to an agency in Paris for training.

By the time the dormitories were finished the staff had finished their training and were ready to open the dormitories. We had three times more applicants than beds. I immediately started a waiting list.

Things were going smoothly, until we received an emergency message early one morning and were told that one of the dormitories had burned completely during the night. The news was distressing but Michelle was duly upset. We checked with the insurance company and the police. After several days, we had a suspect—a homeless man named Marcus, who had tried to enter the building and go in one of the rooms. He was apprehended and Michelle insisted on talking with him individually. He was a native of Tuscovia.

The way Michelle treated Marcus was picked up by the local newspaper and made an impression on the entire country. The police brought him over and Michelle spent several hours with him. After their conference Michelle gave him a job on the maintenance crew which included a room of his own. Her kindness to this man, and her treatment of him made an impression on the entire staff. Michelle also talked with Marcus, a second time. Before he went to prison Michelle gave him a cash bonus to start a savings account.

As Marcus was going to prison, he asked to make a statement to the press. He said very clearly that he had become a Christian and wanted everyone to know his decision and hoped they could understand.

After a great deal of negotiating our insurance company paid to have the building reconstructed. We did install fire alarm systems in all four buildings. Michelle got a call from "Ella," the woman who had tried to start the resistance movement and scheduled a time to talk with her. The meeting time was set up. I talked to Michelle and asked her if I could participate in the discussions. At first, she stoutly denied and said that she did not think I was a Christian and did not share the same dreams she had for Tuscovia. We had a long and detailed discussion. (Divorce was discussed as an option.) I could not stand the thought of living without that girl.

The talks with Ella went well and we arrived at a good understanding. Michelle and I worked well together, although I was aware that she got very impatient when I talked.

When we finished in the afternoon, I asked to have dinner with Michelle, and she refused.

I suddenly got very tired, or disgusted, but I could not continue to be a beggar in the relationship. I felt I had had enough, tried long enough ,been patient long enough—-and could not, would not, should not, do anymore. I went back to my room, packed my bags, called the airport, and got a ticket to go home. I left that very night. I did not call Michelle or anyone.

The flight home was a long one. Questions were whirling in my mind: "Was I doing the right thing?... Should I have waited longer?... What if?... What if...I landed in NY and felt good walking on the soil of my homeland. My phone was ringing constantly but I did not answer.

I finally made peace with myself. I stopped the questioning and the doubts. I checked in at the office but did not go to work. I just let the office know I was home. I asked them to respond to all my calls and say, "He is out of town and cannot be reached on his cell phone, He requested that any callers could leave a message."

Michelle finally stopped calling or at least my phone quit ringing. she only called the office twice. I assumed she gave up and quit calling the office as well as my personal number.

I didn't get much sleep. I was in limbo; did not know what to do; should I call: Should I wait?— the questions did not stop.

Finally, finally, BINGO. It dawned on me—-call her mother. I Don't know why I hadn't thought of that. I called before the thought had left my brain. There was no answer. I immediately went to her house. Rang the doorbell and waited forever. Finally, she came, wearing a nightgown and robe. Her hair was disheveled, and her eyes were red from crying.

Her appearance was terrible. I stepped in the door, and she burst into tears. I put my arms around her and led her to the couch. I did not have any idea what had happened and was afraid to ask. I sat and waited and let her cry a little longer. She finally sobbed, "I have not heard a word from Michelle in more than a month. I have called and called and sent messages, wrote letters, and I do not know what to do. I am afraid she is dead."

I said immediately, "Pack your bags we are going to find out." Two hours later we were on the plane. The flight took forever but her mother had calmed down quite a bit by the time we were landing. We went straight to Michelle's apartment.

When Michelle appeared at the door, her mother almost screamed, "What in the world is the matter? Do you know I haven't heard from you...I have been in a panic for a whole month...Please, what is the matter? What have I done to make you treat me this way?"

Michelle was perfectly calm and said, "Please have a seat. Both of you... I will be glad to explain. I have had some strange experiences. I decided to try an experiment. Not an easy one, but I had to find out for myself. So, I moved to Tuscovia and moved in with a native family. I was honestly trying to live their lifestyle. I thought I could. I found I could not. I have learned my lesson. I am not supposed to be and live like they live and behave. I learned fast, let me tell you. I am more than sober now and have learned a very valuable lesson. I thought I could or should live as the Tuscovians lived. I discovered that this was not true.

I am going to be myself—the person that God made me to be–Michelle–and not try to be someone else. I made a big mistake and got lost for a while, but I am home now where I should be." Then she stopped and threw her arms around me and kissed me soundly on the lips.

We all three laughed, decided not to ask more questions and celebrated the entire evening. Dr. O'Brian joined us to celebrate. He was the happiest person in the room.

A crowd of newspaper reporters had stood outside for several hours clamoring for an interview. Michelle insisted that we let them in so she could talk with them. She talked for more than an hour and when she had finished, all the reporters insisted on making a personal contribution, as individuals to the hospital.

That was the first time I had seen Michelle cry since they removed the casts. She thanked them for a long time and hugged everyone who could get to her bed. A lot of healing was happening for Michelle. Just as I had hoped, when the last reporter left, she called me to come over and hugged me and said, "I love you." I was exhilarated when I heard those words. It had been a good while since she had said that to me. The next day both newspapers were filled with pictures of Michelle. It was a glorious day for her, especially since she had not expected the newspaper publicity. She immediately sent for the officials from Tuscovia and posed again with them for the newspapers.

We were hoping that the news would reach the individual households of Tuscovia and be sent out to the entire country, but we had no way of knowing if that had actually happened. To our surprise, Michelle had been named the "Woman of the Year."

We had gathered for a big celebration that weekend. Michelle was an instant celebrity. What a wonderful celebration after all she had endured. It was our hope that the real meaning of the entire process had spread across the entire island. We were thrilled with how the natives responded there.

Alcoholic Father

I was not sure but something inside me said, "Go for it." I had no idea what college was like, but something on my insides kept saying, "Go. Go. Go for it. You will never know unless you try."

It was that and nothing more that put me out on the highway with my thumb in the air, looking for a ride to that town, where I had heard, "They are all Christians there and they treat peopled different." I was not even sure what that all meant but I was already riding in the back of a very large truck that had stopped to give me a ride. Truckers were very kind in that time, nearly always stopped for hitch hikers. I lay down and decided to get a nap since it was a long way to Jackson. I knew that, even though I had never been there.

Several hours later, I awakened realizing that the truck had stopped. The truck driver said, "I'm stopping here but Ted, over there, is going to New Orleans. He'll give you a ride if you ask him. Go ahead and ask him afore he's sleeping and won't answer you."

I walked to the other truck and did as I was told. The driver said, "Git aboard, Son, we will be there in a coupla' hours."

I went to sleep on a tarp in the back of the truck. When I awakened the sun was full in my face. I got up, went to the truck stop and cleaned up. I had written the address of the college I planned to visit. I picked a small school because I thought I would have a better chance of getting in with no money. It was Strathmore College and that was all I knew when I walked on the campus and asked where the president's office was located. Two students looked a little askance at me, but I ignored them and kept right on walking straight to the Administration Building where I was told I could find the president. I found a door with the name on the door, and I walked right up and knocked.

A man opened the door and I said, "Sir, my name is James Anderson. I just graduated from high school, and I want to go to college real bad but I don't have any money and my mamma don't neither. I don't even know where my daddy is, so he couldn't help me neither, so I just wondered if you would give me a job and let me work to pay for the school. I am a farm boy and a good hand, and I can do almost anything. If you would just, please give me a chance, I would be much obliged to you, and I would work real hard too, I promise. I am a good student too, and I make good grades, I promise."

The president was so taken aback he could hardly talk, and he invited me in his office and gave me a seat. He looked at me and smiled as he picked up the phone. He talked to the business office and said, "This is Dr. Fergerson, I want to enroll James Anderson as a student. Send his bill to me each month."

Later I went to the dorm and checked to see if I could find the room I had been assigned. I knocked on the door until someone came. A tall lanky guy opened door and stood there and said, "I already have a roommate. Not knowing what to do, I said, "Are you sure?" The guy closed the door and disappeared. I sat down on the floor and in a few minutes, the dorm supervisor showed up and took me down the hall to another room. I put away the few things I had and then began to look at the stack of books I had brought from the bookstore. Before a minute, I was asleep and as happy as a man can be. Hours later, I got up, found the bath, and took a shower. I was back to bed since it was nearly ten and down for the night.

The next morning, I was up and walking across the campus to the dining hall for breakfast. I had worn my overalls and did not realize they might not be appropriate, so I went back to the dorm and put on a pair of slacks.

Classes were not beginning until the next day, so I read the first five chapters in each of my textbooks. It felt good having at least some ideas of what the course was all about. I remembered my mother suggesting that I do this, but I had totally forgotten her instructions. I decided to take a walk on the campus just to see what it was like.

I walked out of the dorm and found a small group standing by the steps. I walked up and introduced myself to two or three individuals. No one responded. I remembered my mother's caution about student snobbery and walked on to find another crowd. I found a group of guys and had no trouble getting involved in the conversation, so, I stayed just a minute and talked. I felt good when I saw them listening to me and I answered when they talked directly to me. I had not had this same experience with guys in quite a while.

I decided to go back to my room. Realizing one pair of slacks might not be enough for everyday in class, I washed and ironed them and put them away.

I had nothing else to do, so I decided to go and see the maintenance supervisor. I found him in his office and told him I wanted some work to do; he told me to come back tomorrow. I went back to my room, picked up a textbook, and began to read. This is not what I thought college would be. I kept reading for a long time until it was time for the next meal. I went to the dining hall and ate at a crowded table. There was a little conversation but not much. I was very lonely and wished I were at home.

I had been told there would be times like this and tried to make preparations for these same times, but nothing seemed to work today. I turned over and over wrestling with the bed and finally, completely exhausted, I went to sleep. The next thing I knew, the morning sun was shining full in my face. I jumped up and started dressing. I looked at the clock and it was almost time for my first class.

I dressed and was out the door, running across the campus to get to my class. The professor was late, and I was glad. I found a seat, took a deep breath, and was greatly relieved. The professor arrived and the class started. I relaxed and took a deep breath, so glad I was finally where I had dreamed of being. When the class ended I walked out and realized I only needed to go across the hall to my next class.

The entire day went well for me. I introduced himself to two professors but not to others. They were both very busy, but I did not care. I wanted the teachers to know I was there and proud to be a student.

After my class I decided to check out the student union building. As I walked in, I was amazed at the crowd. The building was packed with students. I was very careful with my money because I had so little, but I decided to splurge and get a malt. I got my drink and sat down at a table that was empty. Immediately three girls came up and said, "Thank you for saving a place for us. We have been looking everywhere for you." There was nothing I could do or say, except, "I have been waiting for you forever, where in the world have you been?"

They sat down immediately, and I was glad to have some company. The blonde with long, beautiful hair sat by me and said, "I'm Marie, who in the world are you?"

The brunette next to her said, "I'm Sarah, the nice one in this group."

The third one sitting across the table said, "And I am Elizabeth, the chaperone in the crowd, so don't worry. I won't let them hurt you."

I reached for the check even though I was not sure I had enough to pay it, but Elizabeth said, "Absolutely not, this is our treat. We don't even know your name yet. Were you waiting for someone else?"

I said, " My name is James, and No, I was just waiting for three beautiful girls to come and sit at my table. Where have you been? You are late. I thought you would never get here."

Marie smiled, "We hoped you wouldn't give up. So glad you stayed and waited."

I teased, "Three girls tried to sit here but they weren't pretty as you, so I ran them off. So glad you came."

Everyone was laughing so I kept quiet for a while and listened. Marie asked, "First year?"

I said, "Yes."

. . . .

SHE SAID, "ME, TOO. Can I see your schedule?" I pushed it across the table, and she said, "Good, we have two classes together. Can we sit together?"

"Of course, I would love to!" And I loved the way she smiled.

All of a sudden, my whole attitude was changing. I was amazed at myself and how much different I was feeling on my insides. I had never experienced anything in my life like this. We laughed and talked about the courses we were taking and who we thought our teachers would be.

We talked a little about grades and I said I was going to make good grades because I planned to go to graduate school. All three girls looked at me and began to ask questions that I could not answer. They all three congratulated me for my ambition.

They asked if I would walk with them to the dorm and of course, I was more than happy to do that. We laughed and had fun all the way. I hated to leave these three women! I suggested we meet for a malt the next night after our last class and everyone agreed.

I left their dorm and walked on air back to my dorm. It had been a beautiful evening for me, and I had not expected or hoped for anything so wonderful. I decided to study just a little before I went to sleep. In just a few minutes I heard my book fall on the floor and did not even turn over to pick it up.

The next day my first class was physics and then chemistry. I left both classes in a fog because I was totally lost before the lectures were half finished. I headed back to my dorm and started on both books with a vengeance. I was determined to understand these two subjects. I stopped studying at midnight and crawled in bed exhausted. Before I went to sleep I remembered my date with the three girls. I had completely forgotten about them! I still went to sleep very quickly.

The next day at breakfast I ran into Marie. She put her nose up in the air and did not speak or look at me. I watched to see where she was eating and later went to her table where she was eating alone. I sat down and said, "Will you please listen just one minute?" She turned her head and did not say a word. I waited just a few minutes. She was not sitting in her regular seat ,but I sat in the same place. I left right after this class and went to my second class.

I felt terrible because I had missed the appointment but mostly because I could not explain. I did not see any of the three girls for several days and went back to studying very hard. I finally began to catch up in chemistry and physics. I talked to the professors and they both referred me to their teaching assistants. I met with both of them after all my classes each day. They were of some help, but I still felt very inadequate in those two classes. I read more and more, made notes over and over, but I was still very much behind the professor's lectures. I considered dropping both courses but realized I could not do without them. So, there was nothing to do but work harder and harder. I read past midnight until 2:00 A.M. when I was so sleepy I had to read standing up and even dancing a little occasionally.

I was beginning to understand what I was reading, and it felt so good. I stopped looking out the window and paid closer attention to the professor. One day we had a surprise test in class. I made a grade of one hundred on the test. I was so proud I could hardly restrain myself. I did it, my extra study had paid off. I lost a lot of sleep but finally had the feeling I had caught up with the rest of the class. What a relief!

I looked for Marie and she had her head down and it looked like she was crying. When class was over, I walked down the hall slowly so she could catch me if she wanted to.

She caught up with me and asked if she could walk with me. I said, "Only if we go and have a malt." She laughed and grabbed my arm with both hands.

I felt ten feet tall. It was a wonderful moment for me. We talked about chemistry, and I explained a few basic concepts she had missed. She was overjoyed when we were finished, and I felt like a giant. Marie asked if we could eat dinner together and, of course, I was thrilled to say "yes."

At dinner that night, Sarah and Elizabeth came with Marie. They both were having a hard time with chemistry, so Marie asked me to repeat some of the same things I had gone over with her. We had a great meal with a lot of laughter. I also made some suggestions about their study habits, and they seemed to appreciate it.

When our meal had ended, I headed straight to my room because I knew I had a lot of studying to do. It was past midnight when I finished, and I was ready to hit the hay.

The next day after chemistry class Professor Sartrin asked if I could stay a few minutes. I stood by his desk and waited for him to finish some work. He looked at me and said, "Are you happy in my chemistry class."

Of course, I said, "Yes, Sir, I am learning a lot."

Dr. Sartrin said, " I just wondered if you would be interested or willing to help me grade papers."

My heart jumped inside my chest, and I could hardly breathe, I was so very proud when I said, "Yes, Sir, I would be glad to do that."

He smiled and reached in one of the drawers in his desk and handed me a big pile of papers. I took them and asked, "When would you like to have them back?"

He kept looking in the desk drawers and said, "As soon as it is convenient for you, James."

I was so proud when he called my name. I asked, " Is there anything else, Sir?" and he answered without looking up, so I left the room.

I left the building so happy I felt I could not stand it. I could hardly wait to tell my mother. I called but she did not answer so I ran up the stairs to my room and was in the shower in nothing flat. I did not study, I was asleep almost before my head hit the pillow.

I was up early the next morning looking through the papers that I needed to go through. I have to admit, all of a sudden, I felt important, maybe for the first time in my life. It was strange but I did feel different.

I was walking across the campus to my chemistry class with all the papers I had graded the night before. I walked right in and went to the professor's desk and left the papers there. I was sure everyone in the room had seen me and I felt ten feet tall. I found my chair and sat by Marie.

When the class was over, I was walking to my physics class and a boy I had met, named Scott, caught up with me and said, "Are you grading papers for the teacher?"

I answered quietly and he exclaimed, "Boy, that's great. How did you do that?" I decided it was best not to try and answer. Then Scott turned to me and asked, "Where do you go to church?

I was a little embarrassed when I said, "I do not go to church anywhere."

Scott slapped me on the shoulder and said, "Great, you can go with me next Sunday. Lots of cute girls and nice guys. You will enjoy it. I do and I go every Sunday. I'll pick you up at your dorm. Is ten o'clock OK? Incidentally, Coffee is free there."

We went on to our separate dorms. I was surprised that I had agreed to go to church with him, but I thought, "I can always call and cancel."

The week was uneventful. I found that grading papers took more time than I had expected. I was still asleep on Sunday when Scott showed up to take me to church, but I dressed quickly. He didn't mind waiting a short time. We got to church and walked into an ocean of students laughing and talking; obviously, everyone was having a great time.

I was surprised because I thought churches were quiet and sober faced. Boy, was I wrong, especially about this church. Something strange happened, a girl hit my arm and spilled my coke. She insisted on going to get me another one. When she came back, she introduced herself to me. I was totally shocked when she found out I was a first timer, sat down with me. I was stunned and shocked.

I asked her name and she said, 'Madeline." She immediately asked me to walk with her to her dorm because she had to study. When we were walking, I asked if we could eat dinner together. She said she would be happy to eat with me.

I was thrilled, of course, and asked what her next class was and was happy to find that it was chemistry. When I told her I graded the papers, she hit me on the shoulder and screamed, "Nobody but smarties grade papers." I was glad to hear that, but I did not pretend to be a smarty, so I did not respond.

Two weeks passed, and I went by the dorm to get Madeline. She seemed very happy to see me, and, of course, I was proud as punch to be dating such a beautiful girl.

We went to the Union Building and were immediately surrounded by a group of admirers for Madeline, who had already become known as one of the campus beauties. I got a drink and disappeared in the crowd. She found me and was angry because I had left. I tried to explain but she would not listen. I found out this babe was beautiful, but I told her she was also stubborn, and we laughed. She looked at me in total shock and said, "Nobody has ever said that to me in my whole life."

I said, "Your mother should have told you."

She looked at me in total shock. Her mouth fell open, and her eyes filled with tears. She got really quiet for a minute and said, "Let's walk outside. James, I have been spoiled and pampered all my life. She sat down on a bench. "No one has ever been truthful with me. I am a little shocked that you are."

I sat beside her and began to explain that I did not mean to be rude or harsh and tried to apologize. She said loudly, "No, no, no, no, no... no one has ever been honest enough to tell me the truth and I appreciate it, I really do."

She cried a little and I sat there stunned, not knowing what to say. It was just getting dark, and I think she felt better about crying. I put my arms around her and said nothing. In just a few minutes she relaxed in my arms. We sat there for a few minutes and neither of us said a word.

Finally, she relaxed, kissed me on the cheek and said, "Thank you, thank you, big brother I never had. You are great." I took her to the dorm and said good night.

I went back to my room and started grading papers. I was beginning to realize that grading papers might be more punishment than reward. It sure was taking a lot of my time. I did not know that it was my responsibility to report for work at the maintenance department, so I had waited to be called.

I started grading papers. The maintenance foreman called and apologized. He said he did not know I was grading papers, and I did not have to work for him anymore. What a relief, so grading papers was counted as work!

When I went to pick up Madeline for dinner the next evening, she said she needed to talk with me. We found a bench and sat down. She turned to me and said, James, I am a Christian and I want to tell you about how it happened, that is, if you would like to know."

I answered, "I would love to hear all about it. Please tell me."

She teared up just a little and turned to me and said, "I went to church one day, I had been going for a while and listening. I heard a lot of people saying, 'Jesus is my Saviour.' I didn't understand that word but then one day, I had a feeling on my insides. I talked to the pastor, and he said Christ had come into my heart. I had no idea what he was talking about. But then he said, 'Sometime when God is ready, He comes inside a person and decides to live there.' I did not understand what he was saying except I felt like a new and different person. James, it was almost like I had been born again and I was a new person. It was, and is, strange. Do you understand? Can you possibly? I hope you can."

I had no idea what this gal was talking about and wanted to leave and go back to my room. I told her what I was feeling.

She laughed and said, "My friend, I am not going to bite you, so please don't run away. In fact, I felt like kissing you when I was telling my story." Then this woman leaned over and kissed me solidly on the lips!

I was stunned, by the kiss but also by her story. I could not comprehend what she was talking about. So, I leaned back and listened. Madeline shuffled like she was going to get up, but then she leaned back and said, "I'm so glad you are listening. I want you to have this same experience."

"I do not know what in the world you're talking about, but I am more than ready to listen. Will you tell me more?"

She responded, "I do not know what to say at this point, but I will say more when I can. Let's go and eat. I am hungry."

I said quickly, "Let's go. I am starving!" And off we went.

The dining hall was full, and several people were immediately with us and talking like everything. We listened a while and finished our meal.

After the meal, Madeline said she wanted to talk some more; so, we walked outside and found a bench. She started immediately and said, "I guess the thing is, tell me how you feel about Jesus Christ."

I said, " I really do not know anything about him. I have heard of Jesus, but I really do not know any more than a name."

Madeline, said, "Well I believe He was the Son of God and that he came to the earth two thousand years ago. That is the basic question for all Christians. Do you believe that Jesus Christ is the Son of God, and do you accept him as your personal Saviour?"

Her words were puzzling for me, and I asked, "Madeline, what is a 'Personal Saviour'? I don't understand what those words mean."

She responded, "James, we have all sinned and done things that are wrong. We have broken the rules and the laws of God. Jesus died on a cross and paid for the sins of the whole world—-for every person's sins."

I dropped my head and said, "I don't see how he could do that. He was just one man. How in the world?"

Madeline was quiet a minute and then said, "Because He was God and He was perfect as God's son. He paid for all our sins to make everything right between us and God."

I was quiet for a very long time. I stood up and walked around the area where we were sitting and then came back and sat down. After a few minutes I took Madeline's hand and said, "Why in the world would he do that for everybody. He doesn't even know me."

Madeline responded, " He, being God, knows everyone. He knows everyone and everything about everyone—-not only that ,but He has made a decision to love everyone-the whole world, in fact."

I said, "My head is spinning. We have to stop for just a moment. Number one, my friend, no one has ever loved me like that, or surely I would have heard about it."

Madeline stood up, turned, and looked at me, and she said, "You are hearing it now. That is why I came. It is why God brought us together. It is no accident that we met.

God brought us together so I could tell you this amazing story."

I jumped up, stood still a minute, and then started walking away. Madeline almost screamed, "Sit down, sit down, right now until I finish. This is the greatest news you will ever hear in your whole life."

I said, "My Dear, that kind of acceptance sounds very strange to me. However, I am going to believe you and trust you. Madeline, truthfully, I do not know that I ever really trusted anyone. Hate to say that but it is true."

Madeline was quiet for a moment before she said, "James, do you mind if we pray right now?"

All I could say was, "Please do, 'Cause I need help right now."

Madeline said, "Lord Jesus, when we have no words please give us words. When we do not understand, please give us understanding. We trust you to hear us and answer us.

We thank you in the name of Jesus, Amen."

I was deep in thought, and realized I was very calm when she finished and began to relax. I felt better, I don't know why, but I did. I stood up and said, "I must go. I will call you tomorrow."

I walked rapidly–almost ran–to the dorm and was glad to get to the room. I plopped down in the bed and covered my head with a pillow. my first thought was, "I am through with that gal. She is weird. 'Saviour,' what does that mean?" Before I was aware I had fallen asleep.

The night passed and the sleeping hours gave me my much-needed rest. The morning sun fairly embraced me as I hurried across the room to the shower. I dressed hurriedly and made it to class. It looked like a beautiful day. Somehow I forgot all about Madeline and was focused on the professor's lecture covering new material. Class was over and I headed to the student building for breakfast. I did not see Madeline anywhere and when I asked her friends, I was told she had gone home for the weekend. I was a little troubled that she had not told him but guessed it was a hurried trip.

The following Monday, I saw Madeline in the chemistry class, and we sat together. I told her, "I missed you this weekend."

She said, "Yes, my Dad is in the hospital, he had a heart attack I am told. I went to the hospital, but I could not see him. They were working on him or something. I was really disappointed and decided to get back to school instead of waiting until Monday. I am very worried about him, but Mother keeps telling me he is OK." I thanked her for the report, and I went to my next class, and she went to hers.

I had a busy week with extra papers to grade, and when I called Madeline she could not talk so we were separated from each other the whole week. I was interested in continuing our conversation, but it wasn't working out. I decided to be patient even though I did not want to be. On Friday, without a lot of forethought, I walked over to the campus church that I had heard a lot of students talk about.

I did not know where to go or what to do so I just took a seat in a very large room that was near the door. In little while this woman walked up and said, "Hello, I am Annabeth, the organist here, did you want to be alone, or would you like to talk with someone?"

I said, " I would really like to talk with someone."

She sat down immediately and said, "I will listen, and I have all the time in the world."

I was very nervous until she reached out and held my hand. Then I started, "My girlfriend has been talking to me about being a Christian; now she is busy, and I have ten thousand questions. Her father has gotten very sick."

She said, "I understand. Please tell me your questions."

I said, "What is the first step in being a Christian?"

Annabeth explained, "It is very simple. You just make a decision and say, 'I accept Jesus Christ as my personal Saviour, Lord and Master.'"

I smiled in response, "I can say that with all my heart. Annabeth, I really mean that, I really do." We stood and hugged each other. It was a glorious moment, and I did not know why but it was wonderful.

Annabeth continued, "The next step is for you make it public, people usually do that in church so please let's go and talk to the pastor about the next step. Here is his office."

I talked with the pastor a long time. With nearly all my questions answered, I went to the dining hall and found Madeline to tell her all that had happened. We had a great evening together.

The next Sunday Madeline and I went to church together. At the end of the service, the pastor asked if there was anyone who wanted to identify himself/herself as a Christian, and Madeline and I both went down to the front. Everyone in the church came and welcomed us.

I definitely felt that they were seriously receiving us into the church family.

It was a wonderful experience and I really felt welcomed by the whole church. We later went to the pastor's study, as I had a few questions for him. My primary question was, " What do I do next now that I am a Christian?"

The pastor said, "First identify yourself as a Christian with all your friends and associates; second, begin and read your Bible every day (I suggest you start reading in the Book of John.) Third, attend church regularly and encourage your friends to come with you. Fourth, find a place in your room and make it your prayer place. Put your Bible there and keep it there except when you are reading it."

The first thing I wanted to do was talk to my mother because I had not mentioned any of this to her. I made plans to go home the next weekend and made sure Mother would be at home. Madeline wanted to go with me, but I asked her not to go because I was afraid my mother would be nervous.

I went home and as soon as I entered the door to my home, my mother insisted that I sit down and talk. I was more than ready, and beginning with my first talk with Madeline, I told her the entire story. She cried the entire time I was talking. When I had finished, she said, "I should have told you all this myself, but I was not sure enough of myself, so I just waited." I waited for her to continue but she was very quiet and waited for me to finish. We had a brief prayer and a hug.

As Mother and I finished talking, all of a sudden, I heard myself asking, "Mother, where is my father?"

She said, "I lost contact with him years ago. He was drinking and never stopped and was in and out of jail every week. I have not seen or heard from him in years. You might call the city jail and see if he is there."

I called a number for the city, and they said he had been transferred to a holding tank outside the city. I got a number and called and asked about my father, whose name was James also.

It took a long time, but he finally came to the phone. I said, "This is your son, James, Jr."

He answered, "I don't have no g...d.... son!" and hung up the phone.

I waited a few minutes and called back and explained to the guard who answered the phone, that my father did not remember or know me. He was gone a long time but finally came back and said, "Your father is what we call a 'wet brain' and has no memory. If you want to talk, you must come here and see him, and he may or may not recognize you."

I got the address and talked to Madeline. She was more than happy to go with me. It took a while for us to find the place. It was miles out of town and almost buried in the woods, but we finally found it. We parked and went in.

We were told we would have to take a guard with us. We went down a dark hall and found a dimly lighted cell. The guard went in and said, "Your son and his girlfriend are here to see you.

I heard a man scream, "I don't have no g...d....son!"

We stood for a few minutes, and then walked to the cell and noticed that the floor of the cell was covered with drawings all smeared with chalk. My father was singing at the top of his voice, "The Face On the Barroom Floor." The guard said, "That's the only song he knows, sings it all the time. Everyday."

After I was trying to talk with my father for less than a minute, he slapped me in the face. The guard said, "Always stand back when you are taking to a prisoner."

We started to walk slowly to the door, and I heard my father cursing and shouting s.. of a b...! Give me a drink...that's all I want." We heard him continue cursing as we walked down the hall.

Back in the car, we sat in silence, and Madeline sobbed quietly. I said very quietly, "The pastor said, God can do anything. Do you think that is true?"

Madeline was very quiet and did not answer.

I started the car and began to drive very slowly on the way home. A million thoughts were racing through my mind. I did not really know what I was thinking. After a while, I said, "Well, I am going to give it a try." then I pulled the car off the road and parked.

I prayed, not believing a single word I was saying, "God please restore my father to sanity and health. And if I can be of help, please use me. I will do anything to help, if you will show me what it is."

I went back to the campus and straight to the President's Office. I told him I was withdrawing from school. I told him I was going to dedicate my life to helping my father get sober if I never did anything else as long as I lived.

He wished me luck and said I could always come back to school if I chose. I checked out of the dorm and got the cheapest apartment I could find.

I called and tried to find an AA meeting that I could go to that night. I found one and got up and told my story. Several people in the group remembered having seen my father. (They remembered, "The Face on the Barroom Floor") No one had seen him recently and I knew why but did not say anything.

The next day I went to that filthy jail on the outskirts of town and asked for a job. The man told me they only paid minimum wage and I said that was OK. I talked to Madeline later that night and told her what I had done. She strongly disagreed but it did not matter. I was determined and not counting the cost. I also called Mother and she was terribly disappointed that I had left school. No one seemed to agree with me, but I was trusting in God, and if he did not help, I figured nobody could or would. Madeline cautioned me about "bargaining with God" and I tried to be careful to avoid that.

The next day when I was cleaning the hallway, I thought my father recognized me, so I quickly moved to another spot to get out of sight. The fact that he recognized me was encouraging, but I did not get close to that cell for a while because I did not want him to know I was working there.

I worked hard several weeks, and the warden really grew to like and trust me. One day, when there was an especially good meal, I took my father's tray to his cell. He did not recognize me or say anything to me personally. I was glad because I considered myself to be a problem for him. I got a surprise when I went to church and several people more said, "We are praying for your father." It felt as if someone had wrapped me in a warm blanket. I really felt loved and accepted at the campus church.

I prayed almost constantly for my father's health and recovery. I even wondered if God got tired of my prayers. I tried not to get in a bargaining position with God as Madeline had warned me. I was tempted to say, "God take me, but heal my father" and tried to avoid that pitfall.

I had the nicest surprise one morning when I was cleaning his cell and I heard my father say, "You didn't clean that spot over there." I was thrilled that he spoke to me even in that way.

I decided on my own to bring some more chalk because his were all broken and some were crushed on the floor. I brought them and left them on the windowsill without saying anything. The next day, I noticed that several had been smashed on the floor, but I acted as if I didn't see it.

One day, I suddenly remembered that Mother said Daddy painted in oils. I had completely forgotten her words. I bought some oils and a few small canvases and left them in the room where the TV was left on nearly all the time. I watched for several days and could not tell that they had been touched. I was beginning to think that maybe I should move them, but I decided to leave them there on the TV.

More than a week passed, and I could not tell that the paints had been touched.

But then...the miracle! I went to clean the cell after a long weekend holiday and found that all the canvasses had been used. I did not dare say anything or act like I had noticed. I did buy another small block of canvasses and left them there.

I began to feel that some small modicum of communication had taken place regardless of how small it was. I guessed (hoped) that he knew I was bringing the supplies, but nothing –absolutely nothing– was said in words. I always stood at a safe distance and prayed for him while I watched his every move. I began to have some feelings for him as I prayed more and more. I am not sure, but I think I heard a voice (maybe it was God's) saying, "Don't give up, Don't give up, Trust and pray." I did not know oi God was talking to me or if I was talking to myself but either one is OK because both voices re saying the same thing.

The next night I bought an easel and left it sitting in a corner of the cell. When I came the next day, it had not been touched. Two days later—same thing. Three days later—same thing and I was beginning to think I had better give up. The next night I removed the easel and all the paints and when I came to work the next day he was standing at the door and pointing to the corner where the easel had been placed. I left everything in place the next night. When I came nothing had been touched. I said nothing, looked at nothing, cleaned the cell, and left.

I purposely skipped the next day and when I came back two days later, he was standing at the easel. painting. But he never looked at me while I was cleaning the cell, and I never looked in his direction.

As far as I could tell there was some oil on the canvas.

I did not stay long in the cleaning process and got out as quickly as I could. Before I left, I saw him glance in my direction out of the corner of his eye. I was so pleased to see that. It was the first hint of interest on his part that I had seen in nearly a year.

I did not go to clean the cell for three days. When I went back on the fourth day, he sat on his cot and never even glanced in my direction. I was glad to know he acknowledged my presence and my absence.

The next day I left clean clothes on his bed and on the bed of his cellmate. When I returned a day later the clothing had not been touched by either one. I pretended not to notice, cleaned the cell, and left.

Two days later they were both dressed in the clean clothes, and there was a painting almost finished on the easel. I was thrilled but decided not to say anything. Another day, I cleaned the cell and left, careful not to move anything or say anything that I did not have to say.

I waited a week, the guard took both men out, seated them in the lobby, and turned on the TV. The guard let them stay about an hour, and went back, took them to their cell, and left. It was very hard for me to leave, I wanted to take my dad home, but I knew I could not do that without spoiling a year's work.

The guard and I left the cell and did not say a word, but we noticed that they both watched us carefully.

For the next step, I waited for one full week. I was afraid to take it and afraid not to take it. I heard a voice saying, "Go ahead, take the step." By this time, the guard had become my friend. He and I helped them dress in clean clothes, and I was allowed to take them through a drive-in for cokes and burgers. They both devoured every bite.

On the way back to the prison we drove by our house and picked up Mother. She was afraid to get in the car, at first, but finally got in and sat by me while I drove. I drove around the block and back by our house, but my father did not seem to notice.

I looked at Mother and whispered, "Don't cry. Pray." She laughed out loud and I saw my father quickly turn his head and look at her. I could not tell if there was any recognition. I searched hard for some sign of life or interest but there was nothing. We drove and drove around the house, but there was not one iota of encouragement. We dropped Mother off and drove back to the prison.

The warden checked us in without a word. We went straight to their cell and when we were going into the cell my father's cellmate took me by the hand and led me to his bed.

He turned his mattress back and showed me a large group of little figures he had carved. They were very life-like—of men, women, and children. I shook hands

and he gave me a high five! My father sat on his cot and did not say a word. I pretended not to notice. I could tell he was very jealous, and I was glad to see some evidence of emotion. It was very encouraging.

I went back home and had a long talk with Mother. She reluctantly agreed to cooperate and help when she could but did not give me any great encouragement. I left the prison that night without any optimism. I did not want to go back the next day. Until I heard the words of a song we had been singing in church.

"Trust and Obey." I decided it was a message from God and I made up my mind, once again, to keep going and trying. I went to the prison and did my cleaning. Rob, my dad's cellmate, had carved more figures he wanted to show me. I bragged on them very loudly and showed them to my father who expressed no interest at all.

Back at home, I had just laid down to rest when I heard a knock at the door. I went to the door and my mother was standing there crying. She walked into the room and sat down and said, "My Son, I want to apologize. I have been a bitter, cynical old woman and judged and criticized your father. I am as guilty as he is, for I have been no help. I have asked God's forgiveness and now I ask for yours, I 'm sorry. From now on, I am going to work and pray with you for your father." I was thrilled to hear what she said and decided God was answering my prayers.

I found Madeline and told her my good news. We had prayer and thanked God together. We also went to the church to thank the pastor.

He was very gracious and celebrated with us. I also went and found the organist Annabeth and thanked her. It was a great day for everyone.

Progress with my father was slow, laborious, and tedious. Ten thousand times I threatened to give up. There was something deep on my insides that said, "Keep on, Don't stop." It must've been God. I don't know what else it could have been.

Once more, we decided to keep working with my father.

We did and it seemed like it took years before he was dealing with reality, but it finally happened one glorious day. The pastor asked us to tell our story to the church on Sunday morning.

I stood with my father, mother and Madeline and told the whole story. When we finished there was no applause, but the entire church bowed and prayed a prayer of thanksgiving. After that, there was a period of silence so loud, I had to stop my ears.

The church service was a big moment, but the work did not stop. My father seemed to withdraw after the trip to the church and completely shunned me for two weeks.

Gradually and slowly, he came back to the point where he recognized me again. I was losing hope and thought, maybe this is all he is capable of doing, maybe I should stop, but something, God? on my insides said, "Don't give up. Don't give up." and it kept ringing in my ears and heart.

Then one wonderful day when I brought Mother, he sat down with her on the bed. I was so shocked I nearly cried. I turned and started cleaning the cell and never looked back. When I finished, I walked out and went to the front office. The warden sent me back immediately and I went. They were both seated on the bed, but my father had moved away. Mother did not move. I sat down beside her, and my father came over and motioned for me to move. I left and went to the front office and the warden went back to the cell and brought my mother outside. I felt it had been a great day and Mother and I went home. Mother asked me to spend the night, so I called Madeline, and she came over and stayed the night, also.

Breakfast the next morning was easy, and we left immediately for the prison, Mother insisted she should stay with Dad for a while. The warden left her with my father for a while until we heard her screaming. The warden rushed back and saw my father beating and kicking my mother. He went into the cell, made my father sit down on the bed, and then had mother sit beside him. Immediately my father put his head in Mother's lap, turned around to get on his knees and began to cry and sob while holding my mother. The warden, wisely, stepped outside and closed the door, but we could still watch through the cell door window.. He waited until my father stood up, brought mother up, and put his arms around her.

We all stood and applauded while they held each other. The warden very quickly cautioned us, "It is not over. You should expect relapses from your father." His cell mate had already gone back to bed and turned his face to the wall. We stood outside the cell and not a word was spoken. My father sat down on his bed and put his head in his hands and did not say a word.

We decided that was enough for one day, told the warden "goodbye" and all went home. I was thrilled with every indication of progress, and Madeline and I laughed all the way home.

Just before we drove away, the warden opened the car door, shook my hand, and said, "You are to be congratulated on a wonderful job of doing the impossible. I never thought it was possible, even as I watched you working." I thanked him profusely as we drove away.

In the car, we all agreed to pray and thank God for the entire evening. We acknowledged it was God's work and not ours and started singing, "Praise God from whom all blessings flow. Praise him all creatures here below..."

Progress with Dad was very encouraging to the point that he was released from the facility into my care. He came to live with me, and that change brought a new hope in Dad's life.

One morning I got a call from the pastor. He asked if I had a few minutes so we could talk. I assured him that I had plenty of time. And heard him grow silent for a minute before he said, "Our church owns a piece of property downtown in what is called the "HAY MARKET" district. It has never been used and we have offered if for sale several times but got no offers and was just thinking...Do you think... suppose we...would you be interested in you and your dad opening some kind of free coffee shop on Sunday mornings? Anyone could come by and maybe have a sweet roll or something like that with a cup of coffee and hear a short sermon or talk or something like that. Would you be interested? Or could we talk about this?"

I answered immediately, "I will be in your office in fifteen minutes. There is not anything that I could think of that I would rather do. I am coming to your office, right now,—- right now."

I ran out the door, jumped in my car, and was on my way to the church to talk with the pastor. He was waiting at the curb when I arrived at the church. He jumped in the car almost before I stopped and said, " Keep driving." We drove straight to the building he had promised, opened a door, almost falling off the hinges, and went into a semi dark room with hay on the floor.

I said, "This is perfect. Could not be better. We need a sign." He closed the door. We jumped in the car and were off to the sign shop. We came out with a sign that read, "Good Morning. Please come in. Free coffee and rolls."

I told the pastor that next Sunday I would be there with one of the large coffee makers from the church, and I would buy rolls from the bakery. We laughed all the way to the church where I let the pastor out.

Sunday finally arrived, I was dressed, was there early, had the coffee ready, and the rolls hot on top of the boiler in the furnace room.

We opened the door at eight-thirty and by ten-thirty we had served eight or ten people. I turned off the coffee pot and left just a little disheartened. As I drove home, I kept saying to myself, "Rome was not built in one day, Be patient. Wait on God...in his time...trust and wait...not my time but God's."

When I turned in my driveway I felt better. My dad was asleep in the recliner, so I did not disturb him.

I went into my bedroom and lay down for a nap. I woke up with a start and found my father standing at the foot of the bed looking at me. He smiled; the first time I had seen him smile in years. I moved over slightly so he could sit on the corner of the bed. He sat down and said, "You are wearing the wrong kind of clothes. You need to dress like me. You will scare those people to death, dressed like that. You look like a successful lawyer from main street."

The next Sunday morning, Dad was gone when I awakened. I dressed quickly, jumped in the car, and went to the building. I parked my car around the block so no one could connect it to the building. My dad was asleep on a bench by the front door and there were several others standing waiting to get inside. The door opened and some stranger came out with a huge pan of rolls. I walked up and went inside to get coffee. I came back outside with a pot and served everyone. Several went inside, and when I went inside to refill the pot, I saw one man asleep on the floor in the straw.

My dad had come inside and was washing coffee cups in the toilet. After he finished I sterilized them in the coffee pot which I rinsed thoroughly. The room was almost filled with men. I was so proud of my dad I could hardly contain myself. I looked around to find him and he had disappeared. I looked down the street and he was walking off with four other guys and did not look back one time.

Not knowing what else to do, I went home, and Dad walked in the door and put coins in my hand. He said, "Two dollars and thirty-two cents. We will do better as we go along." Then he went to his bed and laid down and was asleep almost immediately. I stood and looked at the shell of a man who had been my father and I kept hearing the words, over and over, "You must be born again."

There was nothing I could do or say, so I slid out of the chair, got down on my knees and said a thousand "Thank yous" to the man on the cross—

then...

My father kissed me on the cheek for the first time in my life.

Poetry — Scribblings

• • • •

AFTER I AM GONE AND you are reading these words . Do not expect them to make

    sense They did not make sense to me when I wrote them—-John DeFoore

I had written everything I wanted to, or at least I thought I had.

Until I read and re-read the writings and wondered

who in the world had written all those words? I did not recognize

any of those pieces. Then, It came to me that maybe I could do better

if I tried again, and tried harder.

Counting one hundred years plus is just a little shocking, even if you are

"old" like some people want to describe you.

Not that it is important—But that is thirty-six-thousand and five-hundred days.

It is even, in hours,...

Oh well, we won't go there but it seems like a long time at two o'clock, depending

on whether it is AM or PM.

Speaking of time, when I read about the age of the universe, or even this planet

and forget to wind the clock or put in a new battery, things do get just a little bit cloudy

sometimes. When I read that God does not live in the world of time, I am glad.

Can't imagine how old he would be. Any ideas?

Back to my subject, we were talking about an infinitesimally small amount of time, unless... you are waiting for someone...

You could almost say

it is nothing unless you have lived a long, long time.

It was mid afternoon

when I realized

the world had stopped turning

and I paused just a moment

to watch the spin and
the falling
of everything in the universe
that had lost its anchor
and was flying thru space.
And I thought: no wonder
my heart is unsettled, and I cannot think—
with the universe in chaos,
how could I possibly be at peace?
So, I sat down and remembered
what I had on my shopping list
and why I was going to the store.
I turned around and retraced my steps.
I went home and sat down on my front steps
and went over my shopping list again.

. . . .

HOW MANY PLANETS?
How many galaxies?
Or I could ask how many universes?
–Beyond names and counting
–Beyond space and place
And I asked myself, who am I anyway?
And what am I doing on this planet?
Why do I not answer which way...
Which way is the planet moving?...
Before I get up and hurry down the street.
Hurried steps. thoughtless movement.
Forgotten times with those I love...
and long to see...
that are not here
and ne'er more will be.

But on another shore
and under another sun
I know I will see them face to face.
While God smiles and whispers
His promise over and over.
Welcome home, my child,
Welcome home.

That is all.
     Stop– be still now, where you stand,
for I, the Master, speak,
Stop everything, do not move one breath until my commands calls
every being to its place
Stop the sun and the moon
as they circle lonely planet
moving from nowhere
and going anywhere.
Stop the world and all the worlds
until the MONARCH gives the word
to move universes, galaxies, and planets
to their assigned places
Decided long ago with one word
from the will and mind of the Master
waiting to hear his command,
short and strong, "Let there be..."

Did I tell you often enough–
     since you have left–
how valuable you are to me?
how many times I remember you,
for strength when I am weak,
for safety when I am afraid,
for direction when I am lost.
Did I say that enough?
or did I assume that you would know,
or was I so absorbed in my own selfish world
to imagine how much my heart was intertwined
with your every thought and action?
I wonder if I should have told you more,
in words or actions or behavior
or thought. I should have,
more times than I did—
and how I wish I had.
Could I have found other ways to voice the unspeakable,
to let you know the questions rumble around in my brain,
bumping into each other and not pausing to change.
But I know there are not enough words nor languages,
or enough ways. If I knew them all and could command
every thought and find form or meaning or feelings
to let you know so I will sit here and wonder, while you
travel through space to your new home
where you will not need me.
and I wonder, Did I? Did I? — Did...I?
And I wait here stuck in this point of time,
separated from you in ways I do not understand,
no matter how much I stretch my mind and heart,

I cannot span the distance no matter how hard I try,
I still leave myself with more questions than answers
while I struggle to push back the curtains of darkness
and spread the message of light heralded by a boiling sun.
For I am still and will always be man, clay feet and made of dirt
that bore me and shall surely claim my return.
and the limitations put on my mind and heart,
to keep me in my place lest I trespass and walk
on Eden's ancient shores and commit the same trespasses
not knowing, remembering, or understanding the meaning
of these words: "Thou shalt not;" so, I answer from my hiding
place.
Again and again, " I hid so you would not see my nakedness."
And I realize my nakedness has been with me all my life.
No matter how hard I try to hide it behind my pride,
my arrogance, my shame, and my guilt,– my sin and my fear.
Then I face the magic of the truth,
that I have been needing since Eden
and only God can clothe my soul.

WELCOME HOME, MY SON

The day dawned in a glorious burst of sunshine.
It was almost as if I could hear heavens trumpets
announcing the arrival of a new day on heavens shore
while ten thousand angels rushed to bless the new arrivals
with open arms and loving hearts to cleanse the wounds
of martyred bodies whose crippled lives proclaimed His name
with dying breath amid the flame of persecutors fire
and I heard the mighty angels sing with loud and glorious voice
singing over heaven's multitude of saints who sang,
"Glory to the Lamb that was slain."
And then I saw an angel bending low with outstretched arms
to receive the newborn body of my son, while he whispered
"Welcome Home my son, John. Your work is done. Enter now,
the place I have prepared for you. Stand and greet all those
who came before and waited here to welcome you to joy and peace
to life on these eternal shores prepared for you
and all those you knew and loved who chose the Cross
and not the crown, to wait this moment when I could
hold your tired body, and breathe into your new life body
the breath of eternity and life everlasting.
AND NOW YOU LIVE WITH THE STARS
eating breakfast watching planets explode
and stand there watching a new universe
being born every minute
and you talk with all the greats that you admired,
so long in silence while now they quietly
listen to your wisdom, wonder at your intellect, and smile at your
music.

WEALTH—
When I look at the rags of my poverty
and scrape away the dregs of my shame.
When I count the pennies I have scrounged
hiding them carefully, lest a thief would come,
and dream of or beg for more of the less I own.
I sometimes study the wealth and the riches you promised
not only promised but provided if I would only claim,
all I could ever dream of holding in my hands or heart
with every desire and hope fulfilled and more.
I am shocked at the difference between what you offered
and what I was willing to receive
compared to what I refused In the midst of all you offered
LITTLE—
Man with little faith, little hands,
little dreams, little heart, and little life
Starving of thirst while standing
surrounded by a
a dozen delicious
flowing springs of cool water.

• • • •

OH WELL——
I wanted to answer when you called,
but I was reluctant to hear
your "How are you?"
when all I could say was,
" I am OK. After I have just returned

from my own funeral and barely
made it home to fall across the bed
and wash my heart with my tears.
The contradiction between my who I am
And who I desire to be is gigantic chasm
separating my "now" from my "could be"
or "wish I was," whichever voice is loudest.
At the time, my hearing is dull enough
for me to assimilate and comprehend,
thru the static and the chatter of the falling
skies while the universe explodes in upheaval.
So, I turned on the TV and listened to a review
of the news I had heard yesterday or the day before.
Spelling out man's inability to learn from the history
of yesterday's mistakes or tomorrow's fears.
I turned my face to the wall and pretended not to
know or understand the passing of the seasons
or the rising or the setting of the sun and the moon
and tides or stormy seas and sinking ships.
Then my son entered the room with a hearty, "Hi, Pop,
glad you are home," and the universe regained its balance,
the stars retained their orbit, the oceans and the seas laid down.
I was amazed at the authority carried in the voice of my son.
While I watched the sun hide its face so as not to cast a shadow
on the pathway of my son walking barefooted across the moon.

GOODBYE—-AGAIN 7/29/21
I do not know how to count the hours, days, and weeks
since you left me, oh, so alone, while I begged you to live.
The night seemed to go on forever while I prayed for you
to stay with me, but dawn finally came, and I watched you slip away
out of my hands and into the arms of God.
My tears were not enough to hold you on the earth.
My breaking heart did not scream loud enough
for you to hear my hurt.
The days and weeks and years were not enough
to build a bridge that you could cross
the separating river that split our worlds.
The valley, the vale that moved our worlds grows more and more
each day, while I scream and hope that you will hear my cry.
And so, I wait in time for Eternity's doors to open,
and I shall see your face again and hold your hand and heart.
Oh, Time be kind and move the space from me to you
and open doors beyond the skies where time has lost its strength.
And could not hold you tight enough
to keep your life from slipping away.
I tried to hold your body tight enough;
so, your life would not leave you or me.
I could not hold you close enough,
though hard I tried,
and I felt you leaving me
when I begged and begged you to stay.
And so, I let you go
while I stood with empty arms
and aching heart and mind.
But I know you had to go.

And I shall one day come
and see your face and hold your hand,
and dry my tears in your long hair
while we walk the universe together.
My thanks to God in heaven
or wherever you are,
and bless you once again
for giving me life so full.

. . . .

AFTERNOON—-
A torrent of words
Like a waterfall
Poured o'er my brain
In early day sun
Uncalled and unknown
Out of nowhere
Uninvited and————-
and lay on my heart like fallen petals
Not knowing where to go
Or what to spell
It seemed to me they were small eyes
That pierced my brain
E'en tho' I looked away
And turned my back
As if they were not there
Until the burden of their presence
Broke down my wall of strong resistance
Hiding the silence of their shouting
And the weightlessness of their breathing

Till I saw an invisible hand
Sweep them all away.
And heard my empty silence shouting
"And who are you?"
The question would not wait
'Till unvoiced message loud and clear
Thundered thru my hands
Screaming, "Write, write now
So, I can live and see the light of day
Or else my soul will die
Without ever having seen
The beauty and the magic of this moment.

• • • •

MY OTHER SELF

I wondered if there was a reason
You never walked into my room
And said, "Hello" to end the mystery
That shrouds your face and
Makes your name invisible
Even though I have written it
One thousand times or more.
And gazed upon the vacancy
Of your face while reaching
Just to touch your hand.
Was there a reason
You spurned the light of day
Even knowing the depth of pain,
The breadth of agony,
Your anonymity has brought to me.

How did you reason to justify your response?
I did not need to possess
nor control you; I only wanted
To touch your eyes or the tips of your fingers
Or kneel at your feet in prayer.
Why the mystery and the gloom
Left by the unknown and strange
When the light of day carries so many answers
That could end your pain and mine.
With light like sun and words so clear
To erase the doubt and pain
So, I wait for your step
I tear apart the curtains of the night—
So sure, I'll find you there.
But lo the space is empty.
And I wait for one more eternity.

SEA MYSTERY—

. . . .

IT SEEMS THE OCEANS breath
     Has filled my heart
     Since first I stood
     On windy day
     And filled my eyes
     With the depths of your memory
     And the breadth of your breast.
     I tried to tear myself away
     To stifle all the scene
     But knew once more
     You would hold me fast
     As you always do
     When I take the dare
     To drink your cup.
     You fill me still
     In desert places
     Water starved
     Not knowing flood
     Or waves or wind
     That caress my breast
     Leaving lonely sailor
     Castaway on sandy beach.
     Scanning far horizon
     For ship that does not come
     Though long he waits
     But does not know
     The craft he seeks

Is by his side anchored
Loaded with supplies
Waiting for Captain's command
"All sails," the wind is waiting
"Anchors aweigh"
So aging sailor sleeps
Measuring time in breaths
On thirsty beach
And waits and waits for ship
that does not come.

COMPASS—

. . . .

NOTHING BUT SAND
        Covered with dunes
        Piled high like clouds
        Rolling back and forth
        Midst stillness and dark
        Stranger to the ocean
        Rivers all run dry
        Carry no burdens
        no sailors nor waves
        they speak with parched throat
        And sun-cracked lips
        Of yesterday's typhoon.
        Camels on their knees
        No more strength to rise,
        With eyes all glazed and dim.
        Riders all sleeping,
        Nevermore to wake
        To move across the sand.
        Heat falls like rain
        In torrents blotting distance
        With blankets erasing desert sun
        While one lonely traveler
        Staggers, falls, and dies
        Unloved and unknown.
        Miles away and gone,
        A lonely widow waits–
        Warmed by setting sun–

Takes one last look
At empty desert space
And cries.
Not one grain of sand
Still marks the spot
Where last he stood
Beneath a beaming sun
Dreaming of lazy rivers
And crashing evening tides.
His parched lips voicing prayers
Never heard thru desert winds
As footsteps struggled
'gainst desert skies
Looking beyond silent stars.

• • • •

• • • •

FALL—
    I had failed to see
    one hundred trees
    loaded with ten million leaves
    waiting for a signal
    from the wind
    that would tell them
    When to let go and feed the soil that
    gave them life and
    waited for life in return.
    To complete the cycle
    of life and death set
    In motion by God's
    right hand when
    He stood one early morning
    and whispered the words.
    "Let there be…" and there was.
    So, I stood only one moment
    waiting for my call to let go.
    Was I supposed to do that?
    So that I could keep step
    with the rhythm that He
    set in motion
    one thousand centuries ago?

• • • •

THE POWER OF WORDS
    All his life he said,
    I tried
    I tried
    I tried,
    But not one single time
    Was he heard to say,
    I will
    I will
    l will.
    All his life he said,
    I wish
    I wish
    I wish,
    But not one single time
    Was he heard to say
    I did
    I did
    I did.
    All his life he said,
    If only
    If only
    If only
    But not one single time
    Was he heard to say,
    Now that
    Now that
    Now that.
    All his life he said,
    When you

When you
When you,
But not one single time
Was he heard to say,
When I
When I
When I.

THOUGHTS IN THE NIGHT

(OR LATE AFTERNOON) WHATEVER————-
　　　To the butterfly
I SAW YOU——
The first time
You landed on my shoulder.
And I turned.
Only to see you fly away
Before I could
Really see you.
But I knew you would return.
Because my heart was so hungry
To see the beauty of the colors
You carry so lightly
Every line and shape
So delicately placed
And each in its own
Position as if God had
Held the palate and
Mixed every color
All by Himself
And just for me
In that instant
When you flew back
Waited one minute
And blessed my soul
So lightly and flew away.

WHY DIDN'T SOMEONE?

I wish someone had told me.
That I was not here to stay
That in a few short years
Someone else would have my name
And own the place I call my home and make it his.
Why was I left ignorant
Of truth so harsh and real?
And mold or insects
Would cover up my name
Making unreadable more than clear
I laughed at time and turned my back
Only to turn and find that the last laugh
Belonged not to me but to time.
I listened while this scoundrel skipped gleefully
Across a thousand days and never once looked back.
Maybe that is why I never learned the secret
Constantly hidden by one thousand pages without number.
Each one waiting to speak his piece but only to the one
Who promises to listen faithfully with closed lips
And folded hands waiting to hear the secret of the mystery.

I stood and stared at the immensity of the stones
behind which I knew there was hidden by my—"what ifs"
Deeply buried inside the fortress of possibility/probability
a bastion prison barred by doors with locks closed by rust
and days with hours that could not be undone.
Even when I added a word and included words like,
he, she, and even I, which I knew surely would open all the doors.
To my surprise they did not budge one single inch
I barely whispered for fear they would fall and then again.
That moment hiding behind a wall of volumes,
I saw, barely visible —————-beyond the spines in, the stack
A huge parade led by
"I dids"
"I knews"
"I coulds"
"Nothin' to it"
"Piece of cake"
"Way to go ,man." and ...
"It was just as easy as pie." Only to find, I had been listening
to an ancient voice, shopworn and tattered.
That certainly was not mine,
but belonging to someone in the misty past,
Long since forgotten and discarded—who still ruled my life.

It is with heavy heart that I recognize
The times, days, and ways my life
Has been controlled by other people, places, and things
While I skipped down a brilliant pathway.
And I happily picked the daises by the roadside
Without ever a single glance over my shoulder
To learn the lessons from my past
That would have made my journey easier.
I saw the others looking backward
And pitied them for wasting time.
I never once asked why,
Nor did I take the time to look.
But ofttimes at night I wondered,
Then in the darkness I thought and thought,
And one thousand '"what ifs" paraded 'cross my bed.
Strange pictures flashed o'er my mind,
Standing by an aged man so sound asleep.

• • • •

WHEN DID THE RACE END? Not that I knew it had started.
I mean the race between foresight and hindsight,
That so guides and changes the life of man.
With sight so keen and eyes so sharp
He does not miss one turn in the road
Or colored change in the sky,
Even change in the heat or cold in the air.
He is aware of everything but the main thing
For he has counted his heartbeats

While he regulates his breathing
Steps carefully counted to measure something
He calls health without knowing what it is.
Without remembering the number of his days-
Already counted and stored in time's vault.
And lifespan already measured and recorded
By unseen hand that writes in unknown tongue.

• • • •

I DO NOT KNOW THE NUMBER of my days, nor do I care,
For, if I did, I am sure I would be busy
Making unnecessary plans
Or irrelevant statements
To those who would not or did not care
And could not understand because they would all be too busy,
Just like the rest of us counting their own remaining days.

• • • •

LAMPLIGHTER

• • • •

THE DAY HAD BEEN LONG
Lasting twice as long as it should
To get away from myself,
I hastily dashed out of the house
And ran stumbling clumsily down the street.
I paused to catch my breath,
And in the distance
Out of the very corner of my eye
I saw a light so dim and distant

I could barely pick the spot
Where I saw the figure of a man
Climbing down the ladder
After he had put the light atop the pole
And with his bucket
Added oil to feed the flame
Then moved down the street
To the next pole awaiting the flame
He brought faithfully every day
Same time, same way to light
The way home for every human
To find his way to place called safe
When lost alone and tired
Would seek to find his way
And I paused in my journey
Bent my knee and bowed in prayer,

• • • •

"LORD, MAKE ME A LAMPLIGHTER,
    Give me the oil and fire
    To light the path of those
    Who seek at end of day
    To find their way —-home.
    And when I am gone
    May I leave behind me
    One thousand lights
    To brighten the footsteps
    For those who walk in darkness."

Mystery,
How long I have courted you,

brought you gifts, expressed my love,
changed my plans, to open your doors,
so that you would yield your secrets,
until I realized, your doors have no hinges.
They only open one way
and only open for departing outward.
Still, I begged to see your face,
while you turn over and over
to look in other direction
and strangely I stand and wait.

· · · ·

SO, I LONG AND YEARN for that magic hour
on windy, storming rainy night
when I stand there and the door swings open
and I will see your face and beyond.
Into worlds, oceans, mountains, and valleys
that I have seen only in dreams framed with fear.
I will laugh and sing and dance
When I see the empty shadows
behind the forms that I have given
to my fears so they could find body
shape to reveal their nakedness.
Longing, yearning, for one single glimpse
when I look and see your face,
To solve the unknown answers to questions
never voiced for fear they would go unheeded.
So, my search would never end.
And the untold hours of time wasted
while I stood and stared into empty space
seeking, something, anything, no—thing,
for the unknown that clouded my mind

and left me searching hopelessly
for a fantasy without form or shape.
Where does reality end? and
why should there be an end?
That I cannot pull back the shades
of mystery that block my view
cloud my mind and limit my sight.
Who set the limits, and drew the bounds?
T'was a cruel hand that set the limits
and placed a wall where I cannot see,
forcing my sight to stop so that only
my dreams give me stories of the future,
and I tug at the curtains that cover the sunset
enfolding mysteries unknown, unread, unseen,
seeking to open unread mysteries, hidden long ago
by times dusty move that neither knew nor understood
waiting for that new breath we call "tomorrow"
with dreams and hopes before it comes
erased by sadness, regrets, or memories days after.
And I stand, still longing to know the future.

• • • •

YOU LEFT WITHOUT TELLING me, and I looked everywhere.
   I can't find you. Will you please let me know how you are
   I lost count of the days, had trouble counting.
   It seemed some days had morphed into years.
   And the nights refused to recognize their assigned length.
   After you left, the hands on the clock refused to move.
   And the pendulum refused to swing in its favorite arch.
   I waited for the pages on the calendar to change.

My words and thoughts all run together,
And when I looked it was years earlier than I had assumed
The sand in the hourglass no longer flowed as it had in the past.
Just wondered what had happened to the sun so very dim.
Its brilliant glow had faded without prior notice of any kind.
Somewhere the moon lost its way, I guess, 'cause it's gone.
Until I remembered the days, hours, and weeks with you
And heard my heart listening to the music you gave to me.
And thru the darkness I heard your voice, and the lights came
And I could breathe again to my amazement and surprise.
Please if you can read this, tell me you are Ok and that you wait for
me.

• • • •

"DON'T DO THAT," HE cried as I ripped the mask off his face.
 "I hide nothing. I have no secrets. The reason I wear this mask
 you have not finished with today. One day at a time is the rule
 and not until you have finished today do you have the right
 to remove the mask that blinds you to today.
 Finish today's work. Do not leave undone one single task!
 There remains the task you hid from yourself."
 I paused in my haste and looked around for the unfinished tasks,
 and saw my wife waiting for a friendly hug
 and all the children standing in line neatly behind,
 wanting just one minute of my time.
 I saw the old man down the street, homeless,
 waiting for some word that told him where to find food.
 I picked up the mail on my desk and shuffled aside
 one piece, marked urgent and had my daughter's name
 on the return address which I had forgotten.

I met my friend in the hall and once again,
extended my condolences on the loss he sustained.
My cell phone rang reminding me of the meeting
I had promised to chair for a friend.
Then remembered he had done
the same for me one year earlier
I stopped to remember the day.
Then I forgot tomorrow and yesterday
to say hello again to my now
and I welcomed it with open arms,
while yesterday and tomorrow applauded.

I have never known how to deal with death,
Whether it is close or distant. It all seems the same
It is powerful and final, whatever form it takes,
And seems to put a stamp of finality on everything,
It stands and waits patiently for everyman to enter.
Never hurrying, always patient, holding time in its hand,
As if centuries waited and eternity was patient,
Everything, always in its time and in...

• • • •

OH GOD, I REPENT. I confess that many times,
　I have lived with guilt, fear, and shame
　Long after they were gone, and you had forgotten.
　Even while I remembered for no reason,
　Since you had forgiven and forgotten and all
　Of my sins had been erased by the wonder of you
　While I cling to the tattered rags of my guilt.
　To avoid hearing the angels shout at my being God's Child.
　I confess that I loved the poverty of shame,
　Looking ever backward at my sins
　And ignoring the sacred beauty of the cross,
　Living as prisoner to the past
　Afraid of the gift of undeserved love.
　Until in darkest night and blinding storm,
　I heard your silent whisper once again,
　You had told me, many times before
　The message this time, was music to my soul,
　"Lo, I am with you always, even to the end of..."

Oh, how I long to write a piece of beauty

WITH WORDS THAT PLUCK the chords of the heart
    And evoking colors, forms, and shapes never heard
    Or seen by human eye or felt in heart and soul,
    But I am held in place of past by hand so strong.
    Limiting my words, silencing my phrases,
    Until I exhaust the breath that spawned the step
    And climbing over tradition, customs, and habit
    Until new breath forms thought and action Into substance,
    And the dawn comes clear and bright.

• • • •

THE LIGHT OF THE WORLD
    It did not matter how fast I ran
    I could not escape not for a second,
    a minute or an hour, not even a day,
    should I say a year or even ten,
    what comes next when you are measuring time?
    I had no idea, wondering regardless of how fast
    I ran breathless, looking over my shoulder and, and, and
    trying to go faster than I had ever gone in my life,
    I ran so fast, I passed the wind, then the sun, the moon,
    even the stars until at last I ran faster than light,
    Then, stand-in the darkness and trying to outrun the gloom
    the darkness overwhelming me as I tried to dust off the darkness
    from my coat sleeve, only to find I could not shake the darkness

from my heart, my clothing, my soul or my spirit because then,
I saw that moment very clearly, that once I left the light
I had left myself, my being, my person, all there was of me was gone
The staggering truth was that I needed light as I needed breath
and as I turned away from light the darkness turned to me and hit
me,
full in the face reminding me that the light of the world is still...
THE LIGHT OF THE WORLD...

AGE

I was so shocked
Could not believe
How in the world
could that be?
I pinched
myself,
Am I awake?
Someone
please tell me
I made a slight
mistake.
There is a
an error
in the calculation
There is no way
I have lived
that many years
And that number of days
I can't even
count that high
Please tell me it is not true.
Someone made
a mistake in the count?
Good, I though
there had to be an error
in the total
and it could not
possibly be
accurate.

Everyone makes
mistakes
So I guess
that is your mistake
for the day
And tomorrow
I will make
one for me
No problem
I forgive you
and you
forgive me
Nice huh,
everyone
is free
no one fails
What did you say?
thousand???
There was a mistake
really?
The count
is accurate
Who
said that?

It really has been
one hundred
and five years
not really
—thirty-eight thousand
three hundred
and twenty-five
days.
Please count again
and tell me
quickly
there must
have been
at least
one
error
Oh well,
not now.
wait just
one
minute.
we will
think
about that
tomorrow.—
or the next day

Poetry — War

HE CAME HOME—

But his heart stayed there
        on that lonely little stretch of sand
where I buried my best friend
in a scalding desert sun.
As I begged him not to die
and gave him my last sip of water
and that dirty little foreigner kicked dirt in his face.
and I shot him in the back.
Crying when he hit the ground.
breathing out another death,
falling on my knees, to see another death
making me "older than God."
With a heart too old to beat,
and eyes too blind to cry
I stood on the edge of
the universe counting graves,
that had no names and faces that had no hearts.
Why did Cain kill Abel, and start this crazy mess?
which stretches across the ages
touching me a man so dumb
unanswered dreams and foxhole prayers
leaving empty hearts searching for vacant homes
abandoned and alone as I watched God cry.

LETTER FROM HOME

ANOTHER LETTER SAYING still
   I miss you, be careful
   Each night I pray
   God keep him safe
   And bring him home to me
   He read the letter
   stuffed it carefully
   Inside his helmet
   Where it soaked up the blood
   from the rifle bullet
   The next day she read
   The dreaded missel
   From the war department
   "We regret to inform..."
   She could read no more.
   They buried his body
   In shallow sandy grave
   No time for prayer or tears
   Move forward quickly
   Don't dare, don't dare look back.
   One hundred years have passed.
   A lonely, lonely traveler
   noticed a slight indention in the ground
   And walked around the spot
   And hurried on,
   As if it were not there.

I watch the hours like grains of sand
as they pour through the celestial hourglass
and no one stands there counting
I wait and watch and wish
to no avail because no one is here.
I am on a barren desert of drifted sands
that stretch from earth to sky in unending river
that has no beginning and no ending
other than the depths of my heart
bathed in pain and washed in fear.
This is the place where I am
but a place I refuse to stay.
lest I lose all I have worked to gain.
My body is tired, but my spirit is strong
and has heard the bugle call to battle.
I reject the pain and take away its sting,
I will not surrender. I have no white flag
to hold in the air screaming defeat.
I will fight until my breath refuses to warm my body.
I do not know the enemy who hides behind the pain.
But I will find him and tear away the mask
behind which he hides his cowardice.

• • • •

OLD SOLDIER'S LAMENT—
   He's old, he's stooped
   And he's tired.
   He has lost the war with time

fired his last round and missed
felt the warm blood
washing cross his chest
helped his mind escape
taking him home to mother's hands.
Nobody cares
too many years
Too many tears
erased the world of real
But in the back rooms of his mind.
the guns still blaze
refusing to be silent
rockets still fly
Bomb blasts shake the earth,
Like distant thunder in another land
Night skies are filled with tracers.
staccato machine guns cough,
singing their merry songs of death
'gainst the hymns of dead and dying.
The sad and weary wait their turn
to be covered over with earth's warm sod
and chaplain's sober prayer.
Soldier here is your father,
man, you never knew
he never knew himself and he rises,
takes his rifle running straight into battle,
screaming with final gasping breath
"Come on, you guys,
kill the sons of bitches."
and they mark the place he fell
rifle bayonet stuck in the mud.

· · · ·

AMONG THE THOUSANDS that
    covered the hillside
    I never found his name
    among the crosses
    everywhere but none was his.
    I could not believe the price he paid.
    There was no cross that bore his name.
    It was not there, It had to be there!
    Did they look? He was in plain sight
    when he was hit, I yelled for medics
    who never came.

· · · ·

I WAS NOT SURE HE WAS ever found.
    When last I saw his bleeding mouth
    and begged him to get up.
    I knew he had caught one in the stomach;
    I saw him flinch and fall before I ran
    to help him stand. A sort of smile,
    and partially raised hand
    which I kissed and spit out the mud.
    The sky turned black, my friend was dead.
    The thunder rolled across the earth.
    Lightning split the universe.
    Ten thousand voices said, "Turn and see."
    His cross stretched from sea to sea.
    I knew for sure, my friend was home,
    And God had welcomed him.
    and now his name was spelled in gold.

· · · ·

I HATED THAT SNIPER sitting in the tree.
    After I had seen three of my comrades fall,
    before we knew where he was and went to work,
    But I finally saw the beast who shot them down.
    I trimmed the leaves around his hiding place slowly,
    Carefully, one by one I took them down.
    He could no longer hide and do his work,
    I did not see his face but cursed the day that he was born,
    and watched his body tumbling down for sure and certain death.
    It felt so good to see him fall as I counted my comrades
    one by one that he had killed, but when he fell, I stood alone.
    Not one of my comrades returned.

Hospital tent at 2 AM
I saw her walk into the tent,
flashlight in one hand, syringe in the other.
She stopped at bedside three beds down,
I watched her take the flashlight pulse,
and pull the eyelids back before she left
and returned with the doctor,
then I watched her wipe away the tears,
as she held the flashlight and the doctor looked again
and she made a Journal Entry in the chart.
I turned away until I saw two men coming past my bed
with stretcher, open and ready to receive
yet another one whose parents would soon read,
"the President of the United States regrets to inform... "
I turned again, looked under the tent flap,
at the sky and waited for the sunrise.

• • • •

• • • •

I WATCHED THE WAVES and waves of boats
        in the early morning dark sky and black water
        and saw the tracers scream across an early tide
        and wondered how many would return with time
        and setting sun and burning fire at end of day,
        the roar of engines sang their song of water
        coral and silence filling the bowels of every boat
        praying lips and empty dreams swept across the brows

penetrating the hearts across silent lips
till "ramp down," "all ashore," "give 'em hell," "and hurry home"
the coxan's yell all faces turned to face the fire on waiting beach.
Till hours, miles, years, and dreams later
silence covered over the scene of dead bodies on wave swept sands
and all o'erhead the silent stars sang their evening hymn of silence
as if nothing had happened and the world was the same. as always.

I fired in every direction,
yet saw no bodies
and wondered if no one was left to fight but me,
until I turned and saw his feet beside my face,
I could not find his face or make him talk to me,
but we lay face to foot until the medics
came and took the foot away
so, I watched the setting sun with rising moon
as silence covered o'er the beach
and spread like blanket everywhere.

· · · ·

THIS HARD-NOSED OLD general said it years ago
and no one ever found a better way to spell
the hell that really came when men decide to fight
not one of two or families or tribes or even nations
decide to sweep the earth with pain and death.
Not knowing nor caring the name of friend or foe,
but killing maiming cutting stabbing human bodies
not counting pain or sorrow but killing without face or heart,
without laws or reason, eyes closed killing in the dark.
Insanity running amok thru human hearts and lives
till friend and enemy without face kill finally
human hope and reason and hell reigns as war.
I am not sure but as far as I can tell,
it was more than eighty years ago or more
when I fired my last shot and reloaded my gun
to look for more and cradled my knife beside my heart

to fight if needed when the darkened foe of night would come
to kill my sleep and rob my heart of hope while I wait
for dawn that will not come to bring my hope or joy
or pain whichever came to kiss my day until now I wait
for thousands of miles and millions of dreams I stand
and hear those silent footsteps that spelled death and pain.
while the years refuse to erase the hell and I cry and scream
for peace that does not come with dawn when dusk and dawn are
just the same.

• • • •

I DO NOT KNOW OR CANNOT tell but all my friends have gone
they left no word and gave no sign but when I looked at their place,
it was empty no matter how much I called and searched in every
space.
where did they all go and why were there no goodbyes, no "see you
later."
It was so strange for I was only hoping time would pass and when I
turned
they were not there.

• • • •

• • • •

THEY CALLED IT PTSD at first and I laughed and turned my head
while my nights and days were filled with horror, guilt, and shame.
I did not, I could not believe that others felt the same both day and
night

the same when the dawn was supposed to remove the fear and noise.

There is a monster in my heart and in my soul who never sleeps
he never lies down to take a rest but waits for me to make the move.
Nighttime comes to drive me to my bed and sunny day bidding
drives me further still to the fangs of a monster that invades my life.
I fight him, I curse him, I kill him and walk away looking backward
to make sure he is dead and cannot follow frighten or hurt me anymore
and then he is there in all his holy sorrow to spoil my every hour of rest,
I curse, I fight, I run, I scream yet none of my antics frightens him away.
And then I found his hiding place and looked and looked for rest.
He hides in the scars within my brain and spreads his scaley claws
back and forth against the walls, until my brain is tired and longs for rest.
He roars and thunders loud and long and takes my peace away.

LETTER FROM HOME
Another letter saying still
I miss you, be careful
Each night I pray
God keep him safe
And bring him home to me
He read the letter
stuffed it carefully
Inside his helmet
Where it soaked up the blood
from the rifle bullet
The next day she read
The dreaded missel
From the war department
"We regret to inform…"
She could read no more.
They buried his body
In shallow sandy grave
No time for prayer or tears
Move forward quickly
Don't dare, don't dare, look back
One hundred years have passed
A lonely, lonely traveler
noticed a slight indention in the ground
And walked around the spot
And hurried on,
As if it were not there.

FIRE FIGHT

• • • •

DON'T LOOK BACK.
   It's done.
   The last shovel full
   is patted down
   And safe to keep
   The insects out
   Allowing only brief
   Memories or pictures
   To emerge and disturb
   The sleep of those
   Who marched away
   No backward glance.
   And wondered when
   The time would come
   When other shovels
   Would do the task
   And cover over
   with sod his form
   Then walk away
   To face the curse
   of other guns that
   Would do their task
   And cover the dreams
   Of two broken hearts.

• • • •

UNANSWERED LETTER
    Another letter saying, "Still
    I miss you. Be careful.
    Each night I pray
    God keep him safe
    And bring him home to me."
    He read the letter
    Stuffed it carefully
    Inside his helmet
    Where it soaked up the blood
    From the rifle bullet.
    The next day she read
    The dreaded missel
    From the war department
    "We regret to inform…"
    She could read no more.
    They buried his body
    In shallow sandy grave
    No time for prayer or tears
    Move forward quickly
    Don't dare, don't dare, look back

These words were written to a soldier I found dead in the weeds).
(NEVER KNEW HIM BUT FELT HE WAS MY BROTHER)

. . . .

LAST BREATH

. . . .

I KNEW I WAS HIT
     Dull thud in my left side
     Just above my belt.
     Not too bad, I thought,
     Missed my heart
     So, I laughed and breathed
     Until I felt a warm stream
     Flowing down my leg
     And then it happened
     Damn, what's the matter
     my leg won't work
     Did I fall?
     Dust in my mouth
     Medic, medic, where are you?
     Did anybody see
     Does anyone know
     Where is everyone?
     Water, I need water.

Where is the medic
Where is? what was?
Does anyone? Medic?
Why can I not stand?
IF I could just walk?
Shoe is filled with blood.
Mother, are you praying?
Mary Lou, don't be sad,
Guess it had to happen
Just wasn't expecting it today
Turning dark, it seems to me
Sun gone down-no not yet
Why is it dark?
Did not know it was so late.
Dad, I want you to know
You told me to be brave and strong
And I was—I was brave and strong
but Dad, now I am tired.

THERE AINT NOBODY
I followed him into the brush.
I had watched him many times,
while he sped away to avoid the crowd
all those waiting for their names to be called
"I ain't got nobody back there what knows readin and writin."
He stammered as he explained his need to hide.
I felt the pain and walked him back
to guard the prisoner, we had held for days with no relief.
Days passed by becoming weeks.
He came to me with hat in hand and whispered softly
I can read now and write a little while the prisoner smiled.
Hand in hand they walked away.
It was a miracle. We were not surprised that
the prisoner "escaped" and left handwritten
messages for everyone. We also took pride
in being the only unit that had an interpreter.
It was no surprise to anyone that several days
later this man went on patrol by himself and brought
in fifteen prisoners. Everyone cheered for the new hero.
Who smiled with tears in his eyes.

MAIL CALL—-
She's not writing anymore,
Been gone too long I guess,
She warned me but I said no,
Couple of years and I'll be back,
Days turned into months and
Months to years when letters stopped,
Guess she's busy, lots to do,
Women are like that ,Can't expect her
To write every day. She has lots of things,,
You know women's housework 'n all.
Promised she would write every single day,
Don t know why, did she forget?
Didn't want to leave, hated to see her cry,
That last day at the train, I noticed
She looked a lot at all the other guys,
I didn't say nothin, 'cause she had promised,
And that was enough for me,
I will love you 'till I die, my dear,
And I'll write you every day."
Tomorrow it will come, mail is always late,
And her promise will be true as she said,
For I know her true, and the tear drops in her eyes,
When she whispered over and over
"I will love you till I die."
Then the mail man's voice was silent,
No other words split the quiet.
While he waited for his name to be called
Silence settled in his heart
Shouting down the broken promise

Promises from long ago
Gone the everyday from her sweet lips
Faded quick to memories forgotten
Buried deep neath the sandy hours
And time stood still the whole long night
In fox hole deep with muddy bottom
They left him in his hole
The soldier died that night,
Waiting for the mail call and the surety of the thought
His name would be first on the list, tomorrow
In the dreams of this soldier,
She would stand with open arms saying
"Welcome home, I missed you I love you
And I want to be your wife."

I killed him. Funny thing though,
At the last minute and before I pulled the trigger,
I saw his eyes as he stared at me
Knowing I had won and he was helpless,
His eyes screamed a million "Nos" that said,
"Don't do that, don't kill me, for if you do.
Something in you will die,
Save yourself and walk away
Yes, you have done this before
One more time will not help nor hurt,
"But don't kill me, walk away, and go back
Wherever you came from and whoever you are."
I killed him. Got up went back to my safe place
Got in my hole and went to sleep
Last night, I saw his eyes , heard his voice,
Heard his voice, Don't, don't, don't kill
And went back to sleep.
From another company, not my own.
I heard the story of new recruit who
Had gone on patrol and captured two Japs
They spoke excellent English
And told of their families who lived in California
And had been taken to the internment camps.
Their story was so real that the new and young recruit
Let the prisoner go and got a name and other info...
Also, valuable numbers, he thought about enemy strength.
They were hurrying back with the new information
But before they were out of sight,
The Japs shot them in the back.
One lived long enough to tell the story

New orders soon came down , never, never, never
Too late for the new recruit.
One lived to tell the story.

RAMP DOWN—
He heard the Botswanans scream.
"Ramp Down Give 'em Hell"
"Kill the sons of bitches." "Give 'em hell."
And the Botswanan revered up his engine
to stay off the coral–go back–get another load.
While screams of the dying soldiers
Were muffled by incoming tide and wave.
The sun rose high in the sky
And ignored the scene below as unthinking humans
Fought each other to live and die
The blazing sun smiled and wondered, Why do they fight
Rather than try to survive and help each other
To endure life's brief span, it is so short
Why do they make it shorter?
But the boat had already returned with its load
Of human flesh to sacrifice another boatload of bodies
To this unthinking god with no mercy
On an altar filled with never ending fire
While God looked down with compassion
At man's inhumanity to man
Oh Cain, why did you not find a way to deal with jealousy
Why did you not say to Abel, I'm all you have,
You are all I have, Lets work together, I'll help you
You help me, Why did you think for one moment
I must get rid of him, why not, I must help and care for him.?
Did you not know I would follow you example
Did you not ever think or imagine, "I really am my brother's keeper
Or did you even think?
Cain, You did not kill only one human being.

Not in one moment of time and space.
You killed my brother also.

About the Author

John DeFoore was born in a small town in Mississippi. He grew up surrounded by cotton fields and dense forests. He left home at age 17 and went to work with a highway construction group. He finished high school, started college, and entered the Army when WWII began. He served seven years: enlisting as a private first class and being discharged as a major. He was in the infantry and saw service in New Guinea, the Netherlands East Indies, and the Philippines. He was awarded the Bronze Star during an amphibious landing on Morotai Island.

After the war, John was ordained as a Baptist minister and graduated from Mississippi College with a Bachelor of Science degree, and Southern Baptist Theological Seminary with a Master of Theology degree. He did further study at New College in Edinburgh, Scotland, Princeton, Harvard, and the Jungian Institute in Zurich, Switzerland.

He served as a missionary in Alaska for 5 years, then pastored in Mississippi, Alabama, and Texas for more than 30 years. He began his second career as a counselor and international business consultant and retired from this practice at 98 years of age. He and his wife Marion Sue live in Boerne, Texas. He is the father of four sons.

At 104 years old, John spends his days writing and reading. Since retiring, he has written more than a dozen books.